DANGEROUS CROSSINGS

32
51
66
81
107
123

139
151

THE
FIRST
MODERN
POLAR
EXPEDITION,
1925

Dangerous Crossings

John H. Bryant and Harold N. Cones

NAVAL INSTITUTE PRESS
ANNAPOLIS, MARYLAND

Naval Institute Press
291 Wood Road
Annapolis, MD 21402

Photographs attributed to "Zenith" are the property of
the Zenith Electronics Corporation, Glenview, Illinois.

Library of Congress Cataloging-in-Publication Data
Bryant, John, FAIA
    Dangerous crossings : the first modern polar expedition, 1925 / John H. Bryant
and Harold N. Cones
    p. cm.
    Includes bibliographical references (p.).
    ISBN 1-55750-187-4 (alk. paper)
    1. MacMillan Arctic Expedition (1925) 2. MacMillan, Donald Baxter, 1874—
Journeys—Arctic regions. 3. McDonald, Eugene F. b. 1886—Journeys—Arctic
regions. 4. Byrd, Richard Evelyn, 1888–1957—Journeys—Arctic regions. 5. Arctic
regions—Discovery and exploration—American. I. Cones, Harold N. II. Title.

G626.B78 2000
919.804—dc21   00-026344

Printed in the United States of America on acid-free paper ∞
07 06 05 04 03 02 01 00   9 8 7 6 5 4 3 2
First printing

*This work is dedicated to the memories of
Donald B. MacMillan, Eugene F. McDonald Jr.,
the men of the 1925 MacMillan Arctic Expedition,
and their families.*

CONTENTS

Over the past seven years of our writing partnership, the extraordinary story related on these pages has taken on a life of its own. It has insisted in an ever louder voice that it be told. We are very pleased to finally be able to do so.

We found the beginnings of this story in a most improbable fashion. We share a lifelong interest in all aspects of broadcast radio, and for the past decade we have been researching and writing about its technological history. After publishing a number of articles, our first book was *The Zenith Trans-Oceanic: The Royalty of Radios* (Atglen, Pa., 1994). Trans-Oceanics were the most romantic line of radios ever produced and were sought after by explorers and armchair adventurers alike throughout the postwar era. The Trans-Oceanic was also the personal radio of Zenith Radio Corporation's founding president, Eugene F. McDonald Jr. In 1921, McDonald and a small team of associates took charge of a very small radio manufacturer, then known as Chicago Radio Laboratory, and developed it into the Zenith Radio Corporation—later Zenith Electronics Corporation—during the glory days of radio, the 1920s and 1930s.

As we were researching that first book, we literally stumbled over 154 steel file drawers rusting away next to barrels of trash in a closed Zenith plant in Chicago. Those drawers contained most of the personal files of Commander McDonald from 1927 until his death in 1958. Sealed at his death, these unpurged files represent a unique record of the development of the American electronics industry. Fortunately for this story, the only pre-1927 files surviving in those rusty drawers were several relating to the MacMillan Arctic Expeditions of 1923–24 and 1925, which Zenith had partly sponsored. Although only part of the story of these expeditions survived in McDonald's files, the story was intriguing and, as we soon discovered, was at considerable variance with the "facts" about these expeditions contained in numerous published sources.

As we began research for our second book, *Zenith Radio: The Early Years, 1919–1935* (Atglen, Pa., 1997), we were contacted by Virginia Glendening, the daughter of Cdr. M. A. Schur, USN, one of the navy aviators on the 1925 expedition. Her father's papers contained more of this story, along with a treasure trove of black-and-white photographs. At that point, we were hooked. We traveled to the Peary-MacMillan Arctic Museum and the Hawthorne-Longfellow Library at Bowdoin College, Brunswick, Maine, to read the meticulously kept personal diaries of Donald B. MacMillan. We walked the decks of his Arctic schooner *Bowdoin,* now in service at the Maine Maritime Academy. We visited the Byrd Archives at Ohio State University to read the personal diary and papers of expedition participant Richard E. Byrd. Eventually, we also discovered the few remaining records of the expedition in Washington, D.C. at the National Archives and the National Geographic Society.

As we began serious work on this book, we had to make very difficult decisions on the appropriate nomenclature to use to describe the peoples and places of the High Arctic. In the middle of the nineteenth century, the people living farthest north were generally called "Esquimeau" or "Esquimaux." By the time of the 1925 expedition, the more modern spelling of "Eskimo" was in common use. Most recent writers have preferred to use the term "Inuit," meaning "the people" in their own language, for Canada's most northerly residents, or "Inuhuit," which translates from the language of northwest Greenland to mean "great and beautiful human beings." We have chosen to use the latter terms in this book.

We also have had to ponder how to identify the various communities and geographic features along the west coast of Greenland. At the time of the 1925 expedition, most features in West Greenland (the southern two-thirds of the west coast of Greenland) were referred to by the names given them by the colonial Danish authorities. The features of northwest Greenland were generally called names given by English or American explorers. In later years, when Denmark controlled the northwest coast, authorities simply translated English names to Danish; thus, Melville Bay became Melville Bugt, and so on. As the inhabitants of Greenland have taken more and more control over their own national affairs, many locations are now called by their names in the West Greenlandic language; thus, the capital Godthab is now Nuuk, and so on. Many geographic authorities are now using the West Greenlandic names.

After a good deal of thought, we have chosen to use only the geographic place names that were in use in 1925. We have made this decision because we have used extensive verbatim quotes from the papers of the participants, which of course used the terminology of 1925. Because these extensive quotations are intermixed with our own text, we think that it would be asking too much of the reader to shift back and forth between the terminology in favor in 1925 and that in use in the present. For similar reasons, we have used the 1925 spellings for names of individual Inuhuit rather than their more modern spellings.

No other scholars have ever had access to the McDonald and Schur papers, and most of the Byrd papers have only been available since 1995. What has emerged from our good fortune is an intensely interesting—even startling—sea story. It is a story of the conflict between three extraordinary individuals: MacMillan, McDonald, and Byrd. Together they formed the uncomfortable tripartite leadership of the 1925 expedition, while each held the rank of lieutenant commander in the U.S. Navy.

A huge volume of material was distilled to tell this story, but we have chosen to use a minimum of endnotes to conserve space and facilitate reading. We have included references to key documents in the text and provided an extensive bibliography at the back of the book that details our sources.

The story records several hinge-points in history. The 1925 MacMillan Arctic Expedition was the first to use truly modern technology in the Arctic. This expedition was the first to successfully apply shortwave radio, under McDonald, and aviation, under Byrd, to systematic geographic exploration. It began the process that led from the seaborne, sledge- or bearer-based expeditions of the previous centuries to the aviation-based, radio-linked worlds of Lindbergh, Byrd, and eventually Neil Armstrong.

The 1925 MacMillan Arctic Expedition was accomplished in a swirl of international publicity, contained elements of the intense conflict between the army and navy in the twenties, had some impact on the court-martial of the army's leading aviator, Col. Billy Mitchell, and played a key role in the development of the U.S. Navy's fleet communications, which in turn, had great influence on the development of modern long-distance telecommunications. Most of all though, this is a story of a small number of Americans, almost half of them U.S. Navy personnel, who very knowingly and deliberately sailed and flew directly in harm's way. They put their lives at risk, not once, but numerous times, and they were never recognized for it.

This, then, is their story.

ACKNOWLEDGMENTS

Any research and writing project depends on the cooperation and trust of many individuals if it is to be successful. We consider ourselves fortunate indeed to have had the opportunity to meet and work with so many people who were interested in our project. At the risk of forgetting someone, we would like to express our thanks:

To John I. Taylor, Aimee Huntsha, Howard Fuog, and Gene McDonald Kinney, all past or present employees of Zenith Electronics Corporation, and friends, for their valuable assistance in gathering materials and information and for providing us access to the information that got us started on this project;

To the staffs of the following libraries: the Broadcast Pioneers Library, University of Maryland, College Park, Maryland; the Richard E. Byrd Archives of the Byrd Polar Research Center, Ohio State University, Columbus, Ohio; the Center For Research Libraries, University of Chicago, Chicago, Illinois; the Captain John Smith Library, Christopher Newport University, Newport News, Virginia; the David Sarnoff Research Center, Princeton, New Jersey; the Edmun Low Library, Oklahoma State University, Stillwater, Oklahoma; the Harold Washington Library, Chicago, Illinois; the Hawthorne-Longfellow Library and the Peary-MacMillan Arctic Museum at Bowdoin College, Maine; the Linda Hall Library, Kansas City, Missouri; the Mariners' Museum Library, Newport News, Virginia; the National Association of Broadcasters Library, Washington, D.C.; the Ohio State University Library, Columbus, Ohio; the Regent University Library, Norfolk, Virginia; the Susillo Library, University of Washington, Seattle, Washington; the Texas Christian Library, Fort Worth, Texas; the National Archives, Washington, D.C.; the University Library, Washington State University, Pullman, Washington; and the myriad of libraries researched through the Interlibrary Loan System;

To the staffs of the Danish Polar Center, Kobenhavn, Denmark; the Maine Maritime Academy, Castine, Maine; the American Radio Relay League, Newington, Connecticut; the National Geographic Society, Washington, D.C.; and the Air Force Museum, Wright-Patterson Air Force Base, Dayton, Ohio;

To Dr. Raymond Goerler, archivist, Ohio State University Byrd Polar Research Center; Duane J. Reed, archivist, chief, Special Collections Directorate, Academy Libraries, U.S. Air Force Academy; Mary Ann MacMillan, National Geographic Society, who provided us with valuable access and information; and to Teri Livsey, coordinator, the Oklahoma State University Photographic Laboratory, who performed miracles on the images;

To Dr. Susan A. Kaplan, director, and Dr. Genevieve LeMoine, curator, The Peary-MacMillan Arctic Museum, Bowdoin College, a special thanks for reading and proofing our manuscript and for offering excellent editorial insights and encouragement;

To the late Mrs. M. A. (Virginia) Schur, who so lovingly organized and preserved her husband's extensive collection of photographs and documents, and special thanks to Virginia Schur Glendening, for providing us with her father's expedition material, flight log, and maps, and many excellent photographs;

To Christopher Newport University, especially Dean George Webb, for providing support for portions of this project;

To Patricia Kennedy, our copy editor, whose keen eye and calm professionalism saved us and our English composition teachers considerable embarrassment;

And to the two Lindas, who understand our need to undertake such projects, support our efforts, and still admit to their friends that they are married to us.

Our most heartfelt thanks to all these friends, both new and old; if there are mistakes in the manuscript, they are ours, not theirs.

DANGEROUS CROSSINGS

Early Arctic Exploration

*B*Y THE MIDDLE OF THE NINETEENTH CENTURY, the European age of exploration was winding down. In the four hundred years since Henry the Navigator sent ships south from Portugal, the continents had been fixed in place, the shorelines had been mapped, and all but the most inaccessible interiors and river systems had been "discovered." The latter half of the nineteenth century saw great expeditions mounted mostly by English, German, and Russian explorers who reached the sources of the last great rivers and crossed the few remaining inaccessible mountain ranges, dank jungles, and high deserts of Africa, Asia, and South America. As that century waned, the attention of governments, explorers, and the general public turned to the last and most difficult task: polar exploration. The Arctic was the initial focus of this attention. Finding a useful Northwest Passage, crossing the great Inland Ice of Greenland, exploring the Polar Sea, and, above all, reaching the North Pole, became all-consuming goals for several generations of governments and explorers.

The great Norse sailors at the end of the first millennium were the first

Europeans to explore the Arctic. Most authorities date formal exploration as having begun soon after the 1576 publication of *A Discourse to Prove a Passage by the North-west to Cathaia and the East Indies* by Britain's Sir Henry Gilbert. The great early navigators of the North soon followed: Martin Frobisher (1570s), John Davis (1580s), and Henry Hudson (1610). In 1615 William Baffin explored Hudson Strait and Hudson Bay and returned to England to report that the passage would not be reached by these routes. The first era of Arctic exploration came to a close in 1616 as Baffin's second expedition reached its most northerly point, 78 degrees north latitude, by sailing north through Davis Strait, only to be stopped by solid ice at the entrance to Smith Sound. Baffin returned to report to his sponsors in London that it was useless to continue to search for the passage, and though minor expeditions would continue sporadically, Arctic exploration entered a two-hundred-year hiatus.

The Second Era of Arctic Exploration

The British Admiralty rekindled serious Arctic exploration in 1773 when it sent Royal Navy Capt. Constance Phipps north to counter the continuing thrust of Russia into Siberia and Alaska. Following Phipps's voyage, the first fifty years of the nineteenth century saw a series of polar expeditions, primarily off the west coast of Greenland or north and east of Hudson Bay. These efforts, coupled with the ever increasing whaling in the region, helped to develop a much clearer picture of northern lands and waters.

This knowledge was gathered at considerable cost in money and lives. Two great tragedies of Arctic exploration occurred two generations apart in the 1840s and 1880s. The first began in 1845 when the British Admiralty sent Sir John Franklin's party into Baffin Bay and through Lancaster Sound aboard the *Erebus* and the aptly named *Terror*. The Franklin expedition was Britain's attempt to forestall Russian expansion in the Arctic and to find a route to the Bering Sea. The Franklin party was last seen alive by a whaling captain in Lancaster Sound in August 1845. Despite numerous search-and-

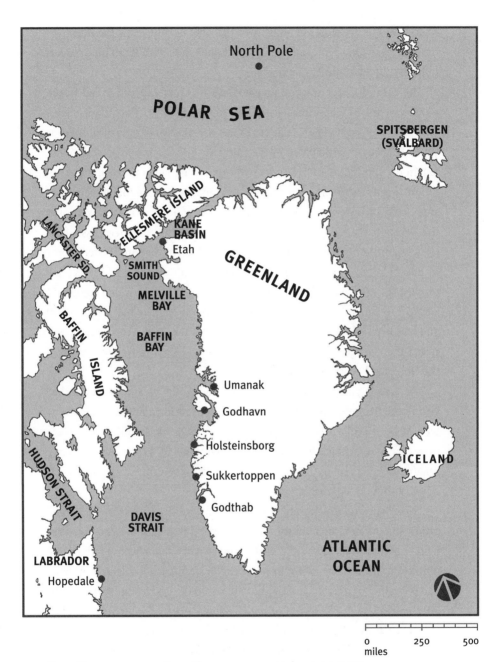

North Pole

POLAR SEA

SPITSBERGEN
(SVALBARD)

ELLESMERE ISLAND

KANE
BASIN

Etah

GREENLAND

SMITH
SOUND

MELVILLE
BAY

LANCASTER SD.

BAFFIN
BAY

BAFFIN

ISLAND

Umanak

Godhavn

Holsteinsborg

HUDSON STRAIT

Sukkertoppen

Godthab

ICELAND

DAVIS
STRAIT

ATLANTIC
OCEAN

LABRADOR

Hopedale

0   250   500
miles

THE GREENLANDIC FAR NORTH AND ITS APPROACHES
John H. Bryant, FAIA

rescue voyages by scores of ships over the next twenty years, the details of the four-year-long agony and deaths of the 128 men with Franklin were not fully documented until 150 years later.

The second major tragedy involved a U.S. Army expedition led to the northern end of Ellesmere Island in 1881 by then Lt. (later Maj. Gen.) Adolphus W. Greely. The Greely party was the most northerly of numerous expeditions that participated in the International Circumpolar Year (1881–82). In the summer of 1882, a promised supply ship failed to reach the expedition, but its members were able to carry on through the following winter supported by summer hunting and reduced rations. The next summer, the Greely party waited as ordered for rescue at their northern base, Fort Conger, until August 1883. They then retreated down the southeastern coast of Ellesmere to meet an expected rescue party at Cape Sabine. When they reached the area in late August, they found a high rock cairn that contained a note informing them that their rescue vessel, the *Proteus,* had arrived early and had been crushed in the wind-driven ice pack. The *Proteus*'s crew had raised the cairn just two months previously and then moved south down the Greenland coast to safety in their lifeboats.

The Greely party of twenty-four men had no boats and faced another year in the frozen Arctic with only forty days of rations. That winter, seventeen of the twenty-four men slowly starved to death, huddled with their mates for meager warmth in their one remaining tent. When a rescue party finally reached them in the summer of 1884, the seven survivors were themselves within days of death.

This tragic and much publicized story profoundly affected polar exploration for the next half century. In retrospect, it is easy to speculate that neither of these tragedies would have occurred had either effective radio communication or aircraft useful in polar exploration been available. Unfortunately, neither of these technical marvels would be used in exploration until after World War I. The lesson of the Greely party was doubly reinforced in 1912 when Robert Falcon Scott's party successfully reached the South Pole and then, as they struggled to reach the Antarctic coast on their return trek, all starved or froze to death only eleven miles from their "One Ton" supply depot.

The great Arctic explorer Fridtjof Nansen made a prophetic diary entry in the summer of 1895. He had left his ship *Fram* frozen in the central Polar Sea and set off on a planned sledge trip to reach the outside world via Franz Joseph Land. His diary (11 June 1895) described the Arctic ice that made surface travel on the Polar Sea so dangerous and so physically demanding:

> Our hearts fail us when we see the ice lying before us like an impenetrable maze of ridges, lanes, brash and huge blocks thrown together pell-mell, and one might imagine oneself looking at suddenly congealed breakers. There are moments when it seems impossible that any creature not possessed of wings can get further and one longingly follows the flight of a passing gull.[1]

As the twentieth century dawned, three great challenges remained for Arctic explorers:

1. To discover and sail the Northwest Passage.
2. To reach the geographic North Pole.
3. To discover what land might exist in the millions of square miles of the Polar Sea not yet explored.

The Northwest Passage was first sailed by the great Norwegian polar explorer Roald Amundsen (1872–1928) in his epic three-year voyage aboard the *Gjöa*. Sailing through Lancaster Sound in August 1903 on his first Arctic expedition, he and his party of five spent most of three years making scientific observations northwest of Hudson Bay. They then sailed west to spend a third long winter north of the Mackenzie River Delta before reaching Nome, Alaska in September 1906. The Northwest Passage had finally been conquered.

Robert E. Peary and Matthew Henson

The assault on the Pole took somewhat longer. Robert E. Peary (1856–1920), an engineering officer in the U.S. Navy, became enamored with Arctic exploration in 1883 when he attempted to cross the Inland Ice of Greenland with a Danish officer. They were unsuccessful and were unable to mount another attempt before Fridtjof Nansen crossed the ice in 1888. Peary then began a

number of expeditions to the north coast of Greenland, headquartering in
the Cape York area near the modern-day Thule Air Force Base. Peary was
joined in each of his journeys by his longtime assistant, African-American
Matthew Henson (1866–1955). In 1900, they established a forward supply
camp at Greely's Fort Conger, on the northern tip of Ellesmere Island, to
serve as a jumping-off point for their first two serious attempts to reach the
Pole. Peary and Henson then began an eight-year-long series of attempts for
the Pole that would finally reach fruition on 6 April 1909.

Peary learned from each of his failed attempts to reach the Pole. Most
importantly, he learned to emulate the hardy Smith Sound Inuhuit hunters
who were superb athletes and dog breeders and, above all, highly skilled
sledge drivers.

In 1906, Peary used his newly constructed Arctic vessel, the *Roosevelt,* as
a floating base camp north of Smith Sound for a major polar attempt.
Despite the active involvement of the Smith Sound Inuhuit on the 1906 dash,
it ended in failure 174 miles short of the Pole. Peary, Henson, and their two
Inuhuit companions did, however, set a new world's record for the Farthest
North at 87 degrees 6 minutes. As they retreated south and then west, paral-
leling the northwest coast of Ellesmere Island, members of the Peary party
saw the tops of what they believed to be high mountains far out in the Polar
Sea to the northwest. They saw these peaks for several consecutive days.
Although a lack of supplies kept the party from turning back to explore this
new land, the peaks were so clear and seemingly real that Peary named the
peaks and the land beneath them "Crocker Land" for one of his financial
supporters. This seeming discovery of "Crocker Land" would fuel Arctic
exploration for the next twenty years.

Peary and Henson returned to New York in the fall of 1906 and were well
received. There was some interest in Crocker Land, but financial support for
further exploration of either Crocker Land or the Pole proved scarce. It took
two years of lecturing and writing to raise the necessary funds for what
became Peary's last try for the Pole. He decided on a much larger party of
"Arctic Men" and a very much larger team of Inuhuit hunters and sledges.
Among Peary's five American companions was Donald B. MacMillan, a
young graduate from his own alma mater, Bowdoin College.

After an uneventful voyage north, they paused at Etah, the most northerly of the Inuhuit villages. They soon were off again, the decks swarming with fifty men, women, and children and 250 of the finest sledge dogs in the world. Capt. Robert Bartlett and Commander Peary forced the *Roosevelt* 250 miles north to Cape Sheridan, where they offloaded almost one hundred thousand pounds of food, sledges, equipment, and supplies. Throughout the long winter nights they prepared equipment and, during periods of the full moon, established forward supply caches on shore.

The final push began on 1 March 1909, when twenty-four men, nineteen sledges, and 133 dogs struck out across the Polar Sea for the Pole itself, four hundred miles distant. As planned, Peary's sledge and team trailed the rest, husbanding their energy. Every four or five days thereafter, one group, made up of an expedition member and two or three Inuhuit, peeled off from the main party. After leaving most of their food with the main group, these smaller parties each returned by double march down the back trail to the south. The last support party broke away 133 miles from the Pole. Peary and his team of Henson and four Inuhuit then had forty days' provisions for men and dogs. They reached the Pole in five long marches, arriving at the ultimate spot on 5–6 April 1909. They camped at the Pole for two days, then swiftly returned south.

When Peary, Henson, MacMillan, and the others reached the most northerly Marconi radio station on the coast of Labrador, Peary's telegram electrified the waiting world: "Have made good at last, I have the Pole."

By the time the party reached the United States, Peary and the entire expedition were embroiled in a series of controversies and accusations, many of which continue to this day. The most newsworthy of these was the announcement by Dr. Frederick A. Cook, a member of one of Peary's earlier expeditions, that he, Cook, had just returned from an expedition that had reached the Pole a full year before Peary. This claim was eventually refuted by two Inuhuit who had accompanied Cook and who testified that their long trip in the area of Axel Heiberg Island never left sight of land. Cook, too, claimed to have seen mountains far out to the northwest in the Polar Sea. He named this landmass "Bradley Land."

With the return of the 1908–9 Peary expedition, only one great goal of

Arctic exploration remained: investigating the large portion of the Polar Sea that was still unexplored. At that time, many authorities accepted the existence of a major landmass in the one- to two-million-square-mile unexplored area northeast of Alaska. Whether it was called "Crocker Land," as Peary had named it, or "Bradley Land," as Cook had called it, such a landmass would have great strategic and possibly great economic value to the country that found and claimed it. One of the leaders in this last great effort was Donald B. MacMillan.

Donald B. MacMillan

Donald Baxter MacMillan was born in 1874 in Provincetown, Massachusetts at the tip of Cape Cod, the son of Grand Banks schooner captain Neil MacMillan. His father was lost at sea in 1883, and he was orphaned at age twelve by the death of his mother in 1886. Young MacMillan lived with two different Provincetown families, the MacLeods and the McDonalds, before moving to Freeport, Maine to live with a married sister. There he finished high school. After graduation from nearby Bowdoin College in 1898, he was employed as a teacher and principal in preparatory schools, first at Levi Hall in Maine, then Swarthmore in Pennsylvania, and finally at Worcester Academy in Massachusetts. In the summers, 1903–8, he was employed as the physical director at an island camp in Casco Bay, Maine.

In the late spring of 1905, Robert Peary, the most famous American explorer of his day, was seeking a young, physically strong, unattached, intelligent young man to serve with him on an attempt to reach the North Pole. Peary tried to hire MacMillan, his son's outdoor skills teacher, but MacMillan had already signed a contract for the following school year and regretfully declined the offer. In 1908, Peary again asked MacMillan to accompany him on what was to be his last polar expedition and MacMillan agreed. The eighteen months in the Far North with Peary changed MacMillan's life forever; he fell in love with northern lands, northern flora and fauna, and especially northern peoples.

If remembered at all today by the general public, MacMillan is recalled as

Donald B. MacMillan in Arctic furs.
The Peary-MacMillan Arctic Museum, Bowdoin College

the third of America's "polar" admirals. This, despite the fact that between his first trip in 1908 and his last in 1954, he led twenty-six separate expeditions to the Far North. Collectively, these expeditions traveled over two hundred thousand miles by ship and over fifteen thousand miles by polar sledge in the service of the Arctic sciences. An informed insight into MacMillan's character was provided by then Maj. Gen. Adophus W. Greely of Starvation Camp. In his foreword to MacMillan's classic book on his 1913–17 Crocker Land Expedition, *Four Years in the White North,* Greely remarked: "Modestly told, MacMillan's story is marked by its fidelity to truth, its accuracy of description, its absence of exaggeration, and its freedom from imaginative efforts to increase its popularity." MacMillan retained his well-deserved reputation for modesty, understatement, and veracity throughout his long career. Ironically, these very qualities may be responsible for his relative obscurity today.

The Crocker Land Expedition

After the Peary expedition, MacMillan returned to teaching and spent three summers exploring Labrador. In 1913, he mounted his first major expedition. With sponsorship secured from three scientific institutions, MacMillan set off for the Far North on a chartered sealing schooner with five companions: Ens. Fitzhugh Green, USN, three scientists, and radio operator Jerome Allen. Expedition plans were to survey coastlines, to make scientific observations, and, in the spring of 1914, to find and explore Crocker Land. A second chartered vessel was scheduled to bring the party home in the summer of 1915.

The expedition put ashore at Etah, one of the main residential sites of the nomadic Smith Sound Inuhuit. Here they established their base camp. In March 1914, after a winter of scientific study and equipment preparation, MacMillan, Green, Elmer Ekblaw (the party's geologist/botanist), and a group of Inuhuit set off for Crocker Land. Crossing frozen Smith Sound and the heights of Ellesmere Island, they paused at the north end of Axel Heiburg Island and then struck out over the Polar Sea. After a monumental struggle through rough sea ice and after crossing many treacherous "leads" of open water, they were temporarily trapped by an uncrossable lead. While camped at the edge of the lead, eighty-five miles out on the ice, they clearly saw hills, valleys, and headlands to their northwest, just as Peary had described. This distant landmass appeared to be in the exact position of "Crocker Land." The sledge party eventually fought their way to a point 150 miles out in the Polar Sea trying to reach this land, which by then had disappeared from view. When rough ice made further progress impossible, MacMillan climbed the highest pressure ridge on a day with a perfectly clear atmosphere to the horizon. He could see nothing but ice in every direction. Crocker Land had been an Arctic mirage.

The sledge party returned to Etah after seventy-four days of brutal travel. They rejoined the scientific party and carried out the program of observations throughout the winter and spring of 1914–15. However, the ship that MacMillan had chartered to pick up the expedition in the summer of 1915 did not appear. After another long winter in the north, no ship reached MacMillan's party during the summer of 1916 either. The wireless, operated by Jerome Allen, proved to be useless above the Arctic Circle, just as MacMillan had feared. By the winter of 1916, the expedition had been without any contact with the outside world for three-and-a-half long years. They had no idea, for example, that a world war had been under way for over two years. That winter, a party traveled by sledge from Etah to southern Greenland to seek news of the outside world and to arrange for a relief vessel for the next summer.

In the summer of 1917, a lookout on the hills high above Etah finally spotted smoke from the *Neptune* as she fought her way north through Smith Sound to retrieve the party. During its four-year sojourn in the Far North, the expedition had many important accomplishments. It had obtained an immense body of scientific observations, surveyed for the first time long runs of shoreline, compiled a three-thousand-word lexicon of the unique Inuhuit language, taken fifty-five hundred photographs, shot ten thousand feet of motion picture film, and traveled ten thousand miles by sledge. The expedition also had proven that neither Peary's "Crocker Land" nor Cook's "Bradley Land" existed. There remained, though, at least a million unexplored square miles out on the Polar Sea to the northwest of Axel Heiburg Island.

Despite the fact that World War I was in progress, MacMillan and his men returned to a hero's welcome in the United States. MacMillan volunteered for the navy and served first as an enlisted man and then as a commissioned officer in naval aviation. After the cessation of hostilities, MacMillan lectured throughout the United States to enthusiastic audiences. His lecture series of 1919 and 1920 had a long-range goal: to raise funds through lecture fees and public subscription for his own Arctic vessel. No longer would the lives of MacMillan or his men be dependent on obsolete sealing or whaling schooners chartered for a season.

The Bowdoin

Peary and other major polar explorers either chartered privately owned vessels to transport them north or, in a few cases, commissioned vessels based primarily on the designs of large sailing ships of the day and strengthened for use in the ice fields. The record of these large ships was mixed; they could carry a large load of men, dogs, and supplies, but many of them were vulnerable to the crushing forces faced in the wind- and tide-driven ice fields. If steam powered, they also tended to be fuel gluttons, often requiring the close escort of a collier/freighter. MacMillan's experience with Peary and with the vessels used in the Crocker Land Expedition led him to conclude that a smaller sailing vessel, much like the Grand Banks schooners of his father's time, would be much more suitable for Arctic work. Being primarily a small sailing vessel with an auxiliary engine and a very large fuel tank, she would be less dependent on fuel supplies. Like Nansen's famous *Fram*, her gracefully curved hull would pop up above the pressures of the ice, rather than be crushed like many of the larger slab-sided vessels.

MacMillan's ship was built by the Hogsdon Brothers Shipyard of East Boothbay, Maine, and was christened the *Bowdoin* after MacMillan's alma mater. Displacing only sixty tons, she was clad with ironwood up to the waterline as protection against the ice. She was considered by some marine authorities at the time to be the strongest wooden vessel in the world. The *Bowdoin* was very efficient under limited power, either ahead or astern, and was said to be able to "turn on a dime." The vessel was paid for by friends from all over the country who purchased shares in her and in MacMillan's Arctic efforts for $100 each.[2]

In 1921, after the *Bowdoin* had been completed, MacMillan obtained the support of the Carnegie Institution for a yearlong scientific expedition to Baffin Island. MacMillan and three companions wintered over, frozen in on the south coast of Baffin Island for ten months. In many respects this trip was a shakedown cruise for the *Bowdoin,* allowing MacMillan to test his design against less formidable ice conditions before again heading toward the Polar Sea.

MacMillan once again took radio equipment north. But, like the set taken on the Crocker Land expedition, it failed to work under and beyond the Auroral Belt, and the expedition was without contact from the outside world for eleven long months. This was the last time that MacMillan would go north without a working radio. Upon MacMillan's return to the United States in the fall of 1922, he immediately set out on another national lecture series to raise funds for an expedition that would mark his return to the Far North that he had come to love. An almost chance meeting during MacMillan's lecture trip to Chicago would turn out to be a pivotal point in his career as a polar explorer.

Eugene F. McDonald Jr.

MacMillan first met Eugene F. McDonald Jr., the dynamic founding president of Zenith Radio Corporation, at a dinner given in March 1923 for MacMillan preceding his lecture in Chicago. The dinner was a private affair attended by prominent naval officers and city officials. The host, U. J. "Sport" Herrmann, was a friend of both MacMillan and McDonald and a fellow yachtsman.

After the dinner, MacMillan gave an informal address and touched on the hardships of the Arctic and his plans for the upcoming expedition to North Greenland. He stated that the greatest problem in the Far North was neither the intense cold (as much as sixty degrees Fahrenheit below zero) nor the privations of short rations, as commonly supposed, but rather the awful solitude. Herrmann asked why MacMillan did not take radio equipment and MacMillan stated that radio would not work north of the Auroral Belt and that there was no room for such equipment on his small vessel. A rather lengthy discussion then took place. MacMillan became quite excited about the possibilities of using the new and physically smaller "shortwave" radios, as described by McDonald, on his planned 1923–24 expedition. This almost chance encounter developed into a lifelong friendship between MacMillan and McDonald and led to several breakthroughs in the development of high-frequency radio.

Eugene F. McDonald Jr., was born in Syracuse, New York on 11 March 1886. He made his first impact selling cars, developing an incentive concept for Chicago auto dealers, and, in 1912, made automotive history when he organized the nation's first finance company to sell automobiles on credit, thus forming the basis of the McDonald fortune. Immediately upon America's entry into World War I in 1917, McDonald sold all his business interests and volunteered for the navy, serving in naval intelligence and based in Chicago.

After leaving the navy in 1919, McDonald briefly managed real estate properties and, on New Year's Eve 1920, had his first contact with radio. He determined that there was far more demand for radio receivers than there was a supply, and he decided to use his aggressive business talents to enter the radio business. In early 1921, he met two young radio builders, R. H. G. Mathews and Karl Hassel, who needed capital to expand their venture. He joined their company, Chicago Radio Laboratory, as director. Under his leadership, the company quickly grew selling "Z'nith" (named for their amateur radio station, 9ZN) radio products. On 30 June 1923, McDonald formed Zenith Radio Corporation, becoming both president and treasurer.

The 1923 MacMillan Expedition to North Greenland

Soon after MacMillan's March 1923 visit to Chicago, both Zenith and the radio amateurs' national organization, the American Radio Relay League (ARRL), were at work arranging for full radio communication to connect

MacMillan's next expedition with the outside world. As McDonald originally had suggested, the new "shortwave" bands being developed for both
amateur and radio broadcast purposes were used. It was felt that radio at
these higher frequencies had a much better chance of penetrating the auroral zone and providing reliable communication in and from the Arctic. In
those early days of radio, all long-distance communication was being accomplished at frequencies that today we call longwave, or low-frequency radio
(15 kHz to 300 kHz), which MacMillan and others had shown to be useless
north of the auroral zone.

Zenith's cofounder, R. H. G. Mathews, was also a vice president of the
ARRL in 1923. He undoubtedly was the person who first suggested utilizing
the large amateur radio community to monitor communications from the
Arctic and to pass messages northward. MacMillan and McDonald worked
closely with ARRL President Hiram Percy Maxim in developing these plans.
Donald H. Mix, whose amateur call sign was 1TS, was selected as radio
operator for the expedition, and a special station license for WNP (Wireless
North Pole) was awarded to MacMillan by the U.S. government.

The role of radio in the 1923–24 expedition was to be four-fold: breaking
the radio barrier of the auroral zone; providing possible lifesaving support
to the Arctic explorers; providing entertainment to the expedition party
through the long Arctic night; and linking the expedition to the news media
through dispatches transmitted by WNP to the North American Newspaper
Alliance. The latter linkage was very important to both MacMillan and
McDonald since each in his separate enterprise needed strong public support. The July 1923 issue of *QST*, the ARRL's official magazine for radio amateurs, explained the critical role that "hams" would play in the success of the
expedition:

> As explained in further detail elsewhere in this article, our job is going to be
> work [communicate with] Mix and get the story from him, and deliver it to
> the nearest newspaper which is a member of the syndicate—the North
> American Newspaper Alliance. It's going to be a tough proposition when the
> weather is bad, and no man knows what success we will have when WNP is
> in daylight for five months nor when she is on "the other side of the Aurora,"

because no man has ever tried those things before. But if any wave can get thru with the power the *Bowdoin* can carry, we think it'll be our amateur waves, and if anybody can copy WNP, we know it will be done by us amateurs of the ARRL.

The rush of preparation and provisioning continued throughout the spring of 1923. As the departure date drew near, Zenith's McDonald and two other special guests were invited to accompany the expedition as far north as Battle Harbor, Labrador.

The Trip North

The expedition was scheduled to set sail on 23 June 1923 from MacMillan's favorite port of departure—Wiscasset, Maine. The two hotels in the tiny town were filled to overflowing and automobiles were parked bumper to bumper around the Customs House, the center of departure festivities. From its steps, the expedition heard farewell remarks from Maine Governor Percival Baxter and from General Greely. These speeches were followed by remarks from ARRL President Hiram Percy Maxim and various other dignitaries. At midafternoon, the *Bowdoin* weighed anchor, stood down the Sheepscot River for the open Atlantic, and turned her bow north.

The passage north went by way of Cape Sable, Nova Scotia, with the first stop of several days in Sydney on Cape Breton Island. From Sydney, the *Bowdoin* headed north, passing to the west of Newfoundland Island and through the Strait of Belle Isle between Newfoundland and Labrador. The expedition remained nearly a week at Battle Harbor, the unofficial capital of Labrador and the gateway to the Arctic. There, McDonald and the other guests returned south by way of a mailboat. From Battle Harbor, the *Bowdoin* crossed the Labrador Sea bound for Godthab, capital of South Greenland, and then proceeded north along the western coast of Greenland and across dreaded Melville Bay to Cape York, the northwestern corner of the island. On 7 August, they arrived at nearby Etah, North Greenland, the northernmost community in the world.

One of MacMillan's primary goals for the expedition was to place a large

E. F. McDonald Jr., Gen. A. W. Greely, and Donald B. MacMillan pose before the
National Geographic Society's bronze memorial plaque, Wiscasset, Maine, June
1923. The plaque was taken north by the 1923 MacMillan Expedition to be placed
at the site of Greely's "Starvation Camp" near Cape Sabine on Ellesmere Island.
Zenith

bronze memorial tablet at Greely's Starvation Camp, located directly across Smith Sound from Etah at Cape Sabine on Ellesmere Island. The *Bowdoin* attempted to cross Smith Sound on 8 August and again the next day, but was stopped on both occasions by the wind-driven ice pack. On the ninth, the Canadian Coast Guard ship *Arctic* arrived at Etah. She also was trying to reach Cape Sabine. As both ships lay at anchor, they received a broadcast announcing the death of U.S. President Warren G. Harding. This is thought to mark the first radio broadcast received in the Far North from the outside world. The following morning, the *Arctic* left to attempt a crossing to Cape Sabine. She, too, was unsuccessful and remained stuck in the pack ice for several days, much to the embarrassment of the Canadians.

On 17 August, the *Bowdoin* sailed northeast along the Greenland coast to Refuge Harbor. There, to MacMillan's delight, all conditions for a winter home seemed ideal: proximity to Cape Sabine, good hunting grounds, fresh water, and near perfect protection from the pack ice in Smith Sound. By the nineteenth, the expedition members had unloaded the *Bowdoin,* taken the sails and running rigging down for the winter, laid the foundation for their magnetic observatory, and begun the first of 286 uninterrupted days of meteorological observations.

It was not until 9 September that MacMillan was able to note in his personal diary the first of many two-way contacts between his radio station WNP and the outside world: "Don [Mix] succeeded in reaching home last night through a man in Prince Rupert, B.C. on the Pacific Coast, a distance of over three thousand miles."

As the brief Arctic fall turned rapidly to winter, MacMillan sent hunting parties out by dog team and sledge to acquire the large meat supply necessary for the men and dogs to survive until the game returned in the spring. The men also insulated the *Bowdoin* with a snow wall that completely surrounded the ship and built hemispherical igloos to act as vestibules over each hatch. The *Bowdoin* party last saw the sun in late October, and the Arctic night began in earnest. Temperatures would drop to fifty degrees below zero.

Radio propagation conditions began to improve as the Arctic day turned into night, and the importance of radio as a contact with the outside world

The *Bowdoin* iced in for the winter in Refuge Harbor, Greenland, 1923–24. Note the igloos on deck that served as air locks over each hatch.
The Peary-MacMillan Arctic Museum, Bowdoin College

became paramount. McDonald, now back home in Chicago, began making weekly broadcasts to the expedition every Wednesday night at midnight Central Standard Time over Zenith's radio station, WJAZ, which had been built specifically for expedition communications. Other early broadcasting stations also produced individual programs for the expedition. Reception conditions were often less than ideal and the equipment, both transmitters and receivers, was rudimentary. The broadcasts did, however, make a very significant difference in the lives of each member of the party throughout that long dark winter. The details of many of the broadcasts from commercial stations were carefully recorded in MacMillan's diary in over twenty entries. The number and extent of these entries indicate how important this contact with the outside world was to the expedition. A typical entry:

23-3954-1

MacMillan is seen here tuning one of the Zenith radio receivers aboard the *Bowdoin* for the 1923 expedition. The specially built Zenith transmitter, licensed as WNP (Wireless North Pole), is just to MacMillan's right.
Zenith

McDonald reads the news over Zenith's powerful radio station WJAZ during one of the special weekly broadcasts to the 1923 MacMillan Arctic Expedition. McDonald had recently returned to Chicago after accompanying MacMillan on the first leg of the journey. The expedition carried Zenith radio equipment and was the first to maintain regular contact with the outside world.
Zenith

> Mon., Dec. 24. At midnight CST our special program began from [the Zenith radio station, WJAZ, at] the Edgewater Beach Hotel, Chicago, Ill. Dr. McWaters [*sic*], Secretary of the Central Graduate Association of Theta Delta Chi, seemed to be in charge. Mrs. Clerk, Mr. Clerk, Lillian and Lettie [MacMillan's sisters] all spoke to us and were heard fairly well. The music was poor. The Eskimos were with us until 3 A.M.

As light returned to the North in the spring of 1924, MacMillan and his party, along with an equal number of Inuhuit drivers, began to range widely by dog team and sledge. Among the many exploratory sledge trips, the most satisfactory for MacMillan was a trip across frozen Smith Sound to place the bronze tablet at Greely's Starvation Camp.

In June, the melting month in the Far North, expedition members began preparations for the trip south. Throughout July, MacMillan and the crew watched the ice in Smith Sound thin and finally break up; however, the ice in Refuge Harbor remained quite solid, holding the *Bowdoin* in its grip. Finally, in early August, MacMillan and the crew were able to break the vessel loose. Using the *Bowdoin* as a battering ram, they escaped the harbor by the narrowest of margins. After a slow and often very dangerous trip down the Greenland and Labrador coasts, the expedition returned home to Wiscasset, Maine, on 20 September 1924 to a tumultuous welcome.

Summary of Radio Activities

When the *Bowdoin* went north in 1923, she was carrying the latest in "shortwave" equipment. It (and similar gear) was called "shortwave" at that time because most other transmissions were on what we today know as "longwave." However, the *Bowdoin*'s radios, called "shortwave" in both radio amateur and radio fan magazines at the time the expedition left Wiscasset, were actually what today we know as "medium wave" or the AM broadcast band. While radio transmissions on these frequencies do travel relatively long distances at night, they are normally limited to well under three hundred miles in the daytime. This limitation was a particularly serious detriment during the long period of total daylight during the Arctic summers and the reason why the *Bowdoin* had such little radio success until the long Arctic night approached Refuge Harbor.

Even with the frequency-based nighttime-only limitation, this first use of radio by an Arctic expedition was very successful.[3] The reception of numerous broadcast stations from North America, especially the weekly broadcasts of Zenith's WJAZ, did much to lift the psychological burden of isolation during the long Arctic night. The amateur-supported communications, although somewhat unreliable due to the relatively low frequency of the transmissions, did provide an important communications safety net for the expedition and relayed tens of thousands of words detailing the experiences of the expedition to the waiting press. Following this successful experiment in radio by the MacMillan expedition of 1923–24, almost all major polar expeditions were equipped with state-of-the-art radio.

MacMillan's lectures given across the U.S. in the ensuing months highlighted the importance of this communications breakthrough. His speech was titled, "What We Northern Men Owe Zenith," and closed with these two paragraphs:

But how different with us, the first Arctic expedition to be equipped with radio! And how different from my fifth expedition, when we were cut off from the world for four years. And can you imagine our feelings upon our arrival at this very place six years later we hear the buzz—WNP—WNP— our call—Wireless North Pole—Wireless North Pole. A small boy sending a message with his home made set from more than 2,000 miles away—from home—he tells us that President Harding is dead. Slowly with bowed heads we stand on the deck of the *Bowdoin* and raise the flag to half-mast—the most northern American flag in the world so raised in observance of the death of a President.

And there under the snow, with only masts and rigging showing, in the depth of an Arctic night, with the wind howling and shrieking over the ice, and up the valleys, and over the mountains, we sat in our electrically lighted warm cabins and heard the music of the operas, of Prima Donnas, the leading ladies, who sang for Zenith by request for us spending a winter in the Far North. We heard the hearty laugh of Commander McDonald who read us letters from home, and who gave us all the important news of the day. There was no time for monotony, for a feeling of loneliness. There was no lack of a topic for conversation. We were happy and friendly and companionable. We could talk with the great busy world to the south. We could talk with far off Honolulu, with ships in the Pacific. We were a part of the world. We were not forgotten. Every Arctic man is deeply in debt to Radio, and I personally to the Zenith Radio Corporation, a pioneer in one of the miracles of the century.

The business relationship between Donald B. MacMillan and E. F. McDonald Jr. was most fortunate for both men. MacMillan tapped a source of significant financial support, especially for the 1925 expedition, as well as a reliable source of state-of-the-art radio equipment. The relationship between Zenith and the most widely acclaimed American explorer of the pre-Lindbergh era was a significant, perhaps crucial, element in the swift metamorphosis of the Zenith Radio Corporation from a small regional radio manufacturer to a leader in the burgeoning American electronics industry. It is readily apparent that McDonald knew better than most of his peers how to use public relations and advertising. The first four or five Zenith advertisements that appeared in the national print media all exploited the relationship among Zenith, MacMillan, and the Arctic. It is a measure of the character of both of these men that their close friendship lasted until McDonald's death, twenty-five years after the business relationship ceased to be important to either.

Planning the First Modern Expedition

*T*HE OFFICIALLY TITLED "1925 MacMillan Arctic Expedition, under the auspices of the National Geographic Society," was the first modern geographic expedition. Previous geographic expeditions had been tied to sailing or early steamship technology for seaborne transportation and had depended on either "native bearers" or Arctic dog sledges for land transportation. The MacMillan expedition was the first to effectively use aircraft to systematically explore large areas of previously unknown lands and seas. Whereas expeditions since the dawn of time had been cut off from communication with the outside world for long periods, the MacMillan expedition used the new science of shortwave radio to maintain almost constant two-way contact with much of the world.

This brief expedition—only ten months long from initial planning to completion—also played a significant role in the adoption of shortwave radio for long-distance communication by military, governmental, and commercial interests throughout the world. The almost unbelievable success of shortwave during the expedition helped to influence the U.S. Navy to abandon its traditional commitment to longwave radio for fleet communications in favor of the much more effective shortwave frequencies. It also served as the training ground and launch platform for America's most prolific expedition leader, Richard Evelyn Byrd.

Along the way, the three leaders of the expedition, MacMillan, Byrd, and McDonald, managed to embroil themselves and the expedition in the then-bitter interservice rivalries between the U.S. Army and Navy. In addition, the expedition would become involved in presidential and international politics and in the conflict between lighter-than-air and heavier-than-air craft proponents. It would even become an element of contention in the court-martial of Gen. Billy Mitchell.

Because of Cdr. R. E. Byrd's apparently conscious manipulations of the truth, the authorship of the plans for the 1925 MacMillan expedition has been falsely attributed to him. In fact, MacMillan conceived the original ideas and almost all of the detailed plans for the expedition by working in an almost equal partnership with his close friend, McDonald.

The 1925 MacMillan Arctic Expedition had its genesis in correspondence between MacMillan and Rear Adm. William A. Moffett,[1] chief of the Bureau of Aeronautics, and in discussions between MacMillan and McDonald, all occurring in late 1924 and very early 1925. MacMillan's initial contact with Moffett was in a 5 October 1924 letter in which MacMillan expressed disappointment that the polar trip of the dirigible USS *Shenandoah* had been canceled. In the letter, MacMillan suggested that the *Shenandoah* expedition should be planned again for the summer of 1925. He ended the letter, "If there is anything I can possibly do to aid you and others in preparation, I would like to do it."

The plan to have the navy dirigible airship USS *Shenandoah* fly over the North Pole in the summer of 1924 had been developed in late 1923. The *Shenandoah,* which was still being built during this period, was modified in a number of ways for the proposed expedition. Admiral Moffett was in charge of the project, which had an additional stated purpose to "seek more land for [the] U.S." The navy also studied the possible use of shortwave radio for the expedition, as well as heavier-than-air craft. Although the planning for the *Shenandoah* venture was extensive, the expedition had been canceled by President Calvin Coolidge in the spring of 1924 when Congress failed to appropriate the necessary $50,000 in funding.

The discussions between MacMillan and McDonald that led directly to the 1925 expedition also began in the fall of 1924. MacMillan was in Chicago several times soon after his return from the 1923–24 expedition. It is most likely that initial discussions between the two men occurred during a trip there to participate in the Third Annual Chicago Radio Show, 18–23 November 1924. Soon after his meetings with McDonald, MacMillan again contacted Moffett on 2 December 1924. MacMillan's letter again expressed his disappointment at the cancellation of the dirigible flight and asked Moffett if he could assist in further naval aviation in the Arctic.

Moffett's reply to MacMillan (12 December 1924) encouraged him to speak out in favor of the navy's involvement in the Arctic, telling him, "I am sure that your well known experience and high standing in the field of Arctic exploration would be most helpful and convincing in furtherance of these ends."

MacMillan returned to Chicago in mid-January 1925 to give a major public lecture. While there, he also spoke about his Arctic adventures over radio station WEBH. Unfortunately, no records of the MacMillan-McDonald discussions during this visit have survived. However, on 22 January 1925, MacMillan sent a three-page letter to Admiral Moffett—on McDonald's personal stationery—outlining an extraordinarily detailed and innovative proposal to explore the two-million-square-mile Arctic unexplored zone with either one or two dirigibles based aboard mothership tenders at Godhavn and possibly Etah, Greenland.[2] MacMillan was very careful to state that he was writing the letter at the request of Cdr. George Isbester, USNRF, Moffett's former aide, and McDonald. Moffett responded to MacMillan on 26 February, calling his letter "most interesting" and speaking to the great worth of such an expedition to science, the navy, naval aviation, and the American people.

In the month between MacMillan's letter and Moffett's response, their plans had changed significantly. They had abandoned the idea of taking

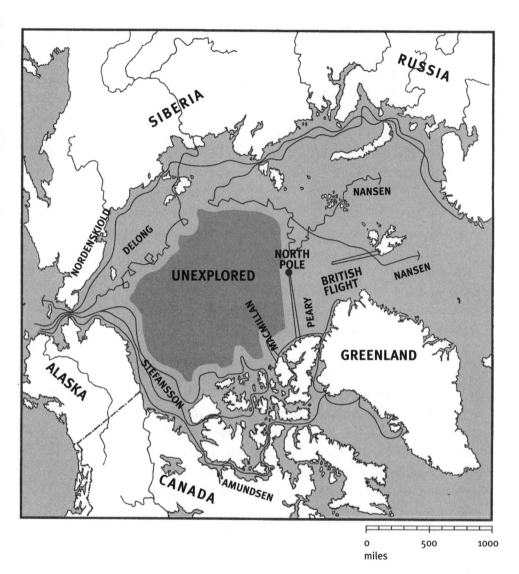

UNEXPLORED REGIONS OF THE POLAR SEA, CIRCA 1925
John H. Bryant, FAIA

Nordenskiold	1878–79	Peary	1906–9
DeLong	1880–81	MacMillan	1913–17
Nansen	1893–96	Stefansson	1913–18
Amundsen	1903–6	British Flight	1924

dirigibles north and focused on fixed-wing aircraft. New York City aircraft manufacturer Grover Loening provided the best evidence of MacMillan's and McDonald's thinking during early February 1924 in his testimony at the court-martial trial of Col. Billy Mitchell:

> I found out [in February] that Commander McDonald and Commander MacMillan were interested in getting some suitable airplanes in Detroit to take up on an Arctic expedition, and thinking that our plane was much more useful, a mutual friend of ours, Mr. James B. Taylor, approached Commander MacMillan and Commander McDonald to interest them in the Loening Amphibian, and Commander McDonald wrote us a letter inquiring as to price and delivery, as they were considering at that time purchasing this plane for use, quite independent of any action by the Government.

It is not possible to say whether it was MacMillan or McDonald who first proposed taking navy fixed-wing aircraft, rather than dirigibles, north in the summer of 1925. However, McDonald, in a 28 February 1925 letter to Moffett, first suggested the use of an "amphibian plane" for the expedition. In a follow-up letter to Moffett on 2 March, McDonald stated, "I have taken the liberty of requesting Admiral Billard to write to the Secretary of the Navy, and your good self a letter covering what he believes can be done if our request for the assignment of a plane to MacMillan is granted."

In fact, Arctic explorers had long dreamed of using aircraft to explore the vast expanses of both polar regions. The Polar Sea, with large areas of wind- and tide-driven ice floes and pressure ridges sometimes reaching sixty feet high, seemed particularly amenable to exploration by air. Balloon flights were attempted in the Arctic as early as 1897, and fixed-wing aircraft were in use experimentally in Spitsbergen, northern Canada, and Alaska by the winter of 1924–25. The only questions remaining were which expedition would prove the use of aviation in the High Arctic and whether the craft used would be fixed wing or lighter-than-air. It should be noted that, in the spring of 1925, Byrd, Amundsen, and others would focus more on achieving a "first" by flying over the Pole. MacMillan and McDonald focused exclusively on exploring the last large unknown area of the Polar Sea.

Today, it is hard for us to visualize that in the 1920s learned men and heads of government and industry could actually believe that a major land-mass might yet be discovered in the Polar Sea. In April 1925 America's "greatest living Arctic Explorer," Maj. Gen. A. W. Greely, stated in a lengthy *National Geographic* news bulletin on the subject, "I am confident there is land of some sort west of Axel Heiberg Island and north of Alaska."

Initial Meetings in Washington

Unfortunately, neither MacMillan's nor McDonald's papers contain the topics discussed during their planning sessions late in January and February 1925. However, by late February, their plans were quite detailed and McDonald traveled to Washington to meet with senior navy officers concerning the coming summer's expedition. His friend, Lt. Cdr. George Isbester, USNRF, accompanied him. Their purpose was to gain the navy's general support for the expedition and, if possible, to obtain an aircraft to accompany the expedition. They met first with Admiral Moffett, who proved to be intensely interested in their proposal. On 28 February, McDonald and Isbester held a lengthy meeting with Secretary of the Navy Curtis C. Wilbur. Apparently Secretary Wilbur was noncommittal and suggested that McDonald draft a detailed letter outlining the plans for the proposed expedition and their discussion. (This letter is reproduced in Appendix B.)

During that 28 February meeting, McDonald gave Secretary Wilbur an extensive briefing on MacMillan's long experience in the Arctic. He related MacMillan's humanitarian efforts among northern people, telling Wilbur that MacMillan was so highly regarded by the "Esquimau" that they wished to become American citizens. He noted that MacMillan was "a professor of anthropology on leave for exploration work" and that he was a lieutenant commander in the naval reserve. McDonald pointed out the long history of the navy in exploration but stated that his purpose was not to obtain funds for the expedition.

McDonald then set forth the goals of the planned four-month expedition. By obtaining the use of an amphibian aircraft, they would explore the interiors of Baffin's Land, Axel Heiberg Land, Ellesmere Land, the interior of North Greenland and the Greenland Ice Cap. He quoted MacMillan's own words: "More work can be done with an aeroplane in a period of days than has been done by all of the Arctic Explorers with their dog teams in the past one hundred years." He went on to say that MacMillan was "strongly led to the belief that there exists a continent" in the one-million-square-mile unexplored area between Point Barrow and the North Pole. He added that MacMillan wished to explore that area by aircraft.

McDonald then reiterated his main requests: that MacMillan be ordered to active duty so that the navy might be credited for the accomplishments of this privately funded expedition and that the Navy Department provide an amphibian aircraft, a pilot, and a mechanic to accompany the expedition, at no additional cost to the navy. He then closed the meeting with an extensive discussion of the strategic interests of the U.S., Britain, Canada, and the Scandinavian countries in any major new lands in the North. Pointedly, he lamented the fact that explorers from these other countries—some with American funding—were making serious plans to conquer the North.[3] (At that very moment, in fact, Roald Amundsen of Norway was readying a polar expedition using instruments borrowed from the U.S. Navy.)

McDonald also stated that, should the secretary not approve the use of the amphibian, "the expedition" would attempt to either rent or purchase one at its own expense. He closed the letter with a plea that time was short and that "we must move rapidly in order to leave in June."[4]

Evidently, Wilbur did move swiftly, but unfortunately no written record of his negative response to McDonald survives. From McDonald's letter of 28 February to Wilbur, it is clear that Wilbur had been concerned about the safety of the pilots and aircraft. Wilbur may also have discovered that the navy did not have any amphibians to loan the expedition. In the spring of 1925, the only amphibian in existence was a single prototype produced for an army contract. The small Loening plant in New York City had just begun work on the first ten Loening production model amphibians, again for an army contract. Whatever Wilbur's reasoning may have been, he did refuse to lend the MacMillan expedition the requested aircraft.

Within three days, the relentless McDonald had begun to appeal directly to President Coolidge. He first sought the support of his own congressman, the powerful Republican Frederick Britten, who had represented the Ninth Illinois District, downtown Chicago, for over a decade. McDonald and Congressman Britten also sought the backing of Maine's powerful senator, Frederick Hale. It was most fortunate for the expedition that Hale, a staunch supporter of fellow New England Republican Coolidge, was then chairman of the Committee on Naval Affairs. In less than a week, Senator Hale had arranged for McDonald to meet with Coolidge in three weeks' time.[5]

In the meantime, unbeknownst to MacMillan and McDonald, another navy officer was attempting to gather support and funds for an Arctic expedition for that summer: Richard E. Byrd, then a lieutenant commander on the navy's retired list, but on active duty.

Richard Evelyn Byrd

Richard E. Byrd came from a prominent and politically influential Virginia family. He served in the Battle Fleet after his graduation from the U.S. Naval Academy in 1912. In 1916, an old ankle injury suffered while Byrd was playing football as a midshipman forced him to retire from active duty. He was shortly reinstated to active duty but in a retired status, and was awarded his wings as a naval aviator (number 608) in April 1918. He served in Canada during the war, commanding two air bases in Nova Scotia. Byrd pioneered the techniques of nighttime landings of seaplanes and developed the Byrd sextant, a navigation device that used a bubble to supply an artificial horizon. Byrd's interest in polar exploration was heightened when he was assigned as the navigator on the abortive transpolar flight of the dirigible *Shenandoah* in 1924.

The earliest surviving evidence of Byrd's 1925 polar plans is a letter from Byrd to Capt. Robert Bartlett, veteran of several of the Peary expeditions. Note that this letter was dated 24 February 1925. In it, Byrd stated:

> I have never given up the idea of flying across the Pole. I think it would be dangerous in an airplane, but not so in a dirigible. Please keep what I am about to say absolutely confidential.

In case the Navy does not send the *Los Angeles* up there this summer [1925], which I very much doubt that they will, I am contemplating attempting to get one of the TC type of dirigibles to Spitzbergen, and shoving off from there for the Pole and back."[6]

Byrd went on to inquire about the details of polar fog, winds, lightning storms, and so on. This letter was written on Bureau of Aeronautics stationery.

On 7 March 1925, Lieutenant Commander Byrd wrote Lt. C. E. Bauch, USN, then serving on the USS *Shenandoah,* again stating that he was planning to take a TC-type airship (nonrigid) to the Pole. He told Bauch that "the National Geographic Society is backing us with $40,000." This statement was not true. Byrd did not even submit a proposal for funding to the National Geographic Society until nine days later. Finally, as with the Bartlett letter, he requested that Bauch "please keep this matter entirely confidential."

On 16 March, Byrd submitted a detailed expedition plan and a formal request for $40,000 to Gilbert Grosvenor, president of the National Geographic Society.[7] In his proposal, Byrd gave a thorough analysis of expedition logistics, stating that the navy had agreed to provide the blimp gondola and many other supplies, while the Goodyear Rubber Company was "expected to supply the airship bag, or part of this." The $40,000 needed from the National Geographic Society was to cover chartering a steamer, the cost of constructing a hangar at Etah, North Greenland, and operating expenses. The next day a letter arrived on President Grosvenor's desk from Admiral Moffett presumably supporting Byrd's proposal.

Two days after receiving Moffett's letter, on 19 March 1925, Grosvenor wrote Admiral Moffett denying Byrd's request for funds.[8] Grosvenor was very complimentary of Byrd's personality and qualities as a leader, but stated that there was no time to adequately prepare for an expedition for the summer of 1925. He added that the chairman of the Research Committee had just left town for a month and that the society already had established a satisfactory program for research and exploration in 1925. Grosvenor closed by stating that he would be pleased to bring the project to the attention of the Research Committee in the fall (of 1925) if Byrd did not find funding for a summer 1925 expedition and "if Amundsen was not successful this summer."

On 21 March, Byrd, then in New York City attempting to raise funds for his expedition, wrote the New York City representative of John D. Rockefeller Jr., Mr. R. B. Fosdick, about his blimp-based expedition, stating that "Mr. Edsel Ford is interested in the project and has guaranteed $15,000. Mr. Marshall Crane has donated $5,000." Byrd also stated that Goodyear was going to supply the air bag at cost, $20,000.[9] This last statement was simply untrue. Eventually, Goodyear emphatically refused to participate in Byrd's expedition. Byrd closed the letter with a statement that the expedition still needed to raise $40,000. It is evident from the letter that Byrd had contacted Fosdick seeking Rockefeller's support for the expedition and that Fosdick had requested further information.

It is important to remember that Byrd had been planning and attempting to raise funds for an expedition based on the TC-type "blimp" dirigible from mid-February until at least 22 or 23 March. Events over the next ten days and Byrd's behavior during that time would contribute to a lifetime of enmity between Byrd on one side and MacMillan and McDonald on the other.

Critical Meetings in Washington

On 26 March, MacMillan and McDonald arrived in Washington for meetings with navy brass and with President Coolidge. They were to call on Admiral Moffett and members of the Bureau of Aeronautics staff, along with Capt. Ridley McLean, director of naval communications, and Rear Adm. J. K. Robison, chief of the Bureau of Engineering, about the proposed experiments with shortwave radio. On 28 March, they held a crucial meeting with a number of officers in Admiral Moffett's offices to discuss the plans for aircraft. They probably also discussed the upcoming meeting between McDonald and President Coolidge. Commander Byrd was present at this meeting and learned firsthand the details of the MacMillan-McDonald plan. Byrd mentioned his own interest in a polar expedition, stated that his plans were by no means complete, and that he did not know whether he would be successful in gaining support for his expedition.

Remarkably, on that same day, 28 March, Byrd submitted to Secretary of the Navy Wilbur, via Admiral Moffett, a very detailed three-page plan for his own expedition to the Polar Sea, now to be based on amphibian airplanes.[10] In this entirely new proposal, he quoted MacMillan's assistant from the Crocker Land Expedition—Fitzhugh Green, now a lieutenant commander—on the ease of landing a "hydroplane" on leads and ponds on the Polar Sea. According to Byrd, Green and others had also advised him that it was possible to reach Etah, Greenland (also his proposed base) through the ice fields as early as 1 July. This faulty advice was to contribute to the ill will between the leaders soon after they got under way.

Today, it is impossible to determine whether Byrd wrote this new proposal, date-stamped 28 March, before or after the meeting with MacMillan, McDonald, and others in Moffett's offices that day. Byrd had just learned that neither the National Geographic Society nor Goodyear Rubber Company would support his blimp-based expedition. In a 4 April letter to his friend and financial supporter, Edsel Ford, Byrd gave his reason for his sudden change of plans: "My negotiations with the Goodyear people were so unsatisfactory that I had to call off the project this year with a TC-type airship. In fact, I doubt that I will ever try the trip with this particular type of blimp. However, I immediately made plans to carry out my project with heavier-than-air craft."

It is impossible to determine at this point whether the seemingly desperate Byrd simply put the MacMillan-McDonald plan in his own words and submitted it or whether he had, in fact, developed this entirely new expedition plan based on fixed-wing aircraft in less than forty-eight hours. Byrd certainly knew that if he wanted to lead an Arctic expedition in the summer of 1925, he had to get a competing plan, placing himself in command, under active consideration by the navy before President Coolidge seriously considered the plans of MacMillan and McDonald.

What is shocking about Byrd's behavior is that he immediately began claiming that MacMillan had stolen his plan for the expedition, charging that MacMillan came to town and "when he found what our plans were, he immediately changed his plans and has now adopted ours." The first example of this claim is a 30 March 1925 letter from Byrd to Bob Bartlett of the Explorer's Club of New York, which was found in Byrd's own files:

> Admiral Eberle [the chief of naval operations] has approved our expedition, and the Secretary also approves of it, but he is going to take it up at the Cabinet Meeting Tuesday. This is absolutely confidential. I regret extremely that the Secretary finds it necessary to take such a small matter up with the President.
>
> Another complication has arisen. MacMillan arrived Saturday, and when he found what our plans were he immediately changed his plans and now has adopted ours. It is most unfortunate, because it does not seem practical for two expeditions to attempt to accomplish the same thing in the same place. MacMillan does not intend to try the pole but he does intend to put down the cache and explore the unexplored region. Anyhow this is the dope, and I can't get my decision from the Secretary until Wednesday.

Even if Byrd's claim that MacMillan had stolen his plans is believable, it is extremely unlikely that the chief of the Bureau of Aeronautics, the chief of naval operations, and Secretary of the Navy Wilbur could each have considered, approved, and forwarded in sequence Byrd's expedition proposal in less than forty-eight hours, as Byrd claimed.

For years to come, Byrd would continue to charge that MacMillan had stolen his plans and that he, Byrd, had in fact planned the 1925 expedition. He first made this charge in "extremely confidential" letters to his backers, and later in more public forums, until this "fact" had entered the history of Arctic exploration. Many people today believe that Byrd was a victim of a conspiracy by MacMillan and McDonald; that MacMillan had "secret plans"; that MacMillan stole Byrd's plans and "compelled" Byrd to join forces with MacMillan. Elements of this apparent charade were found in the laudatory 1957 obituary of Admiral Byrd by Dr. Melville Grosvenor, then president of the National Geographic Society. Commander Byrd's story also appears in the narrative of the 1925 expedition in Grover Loening's book, *Amphibian*, published in 1973, and even in the brief 1997 biography of Admiral Byrd on the web page of the Byrd Polar Research Center.

Meeting with President Coolidge

Completely unaware of what Byrd was doing, McDonald, accompanied by Congressman Britten, met for about an hour with recently elected President Calvin Coolidge on either Sunday, 29 March or Monday, 30 March. Unfortunately, no record of the details of that meeting has been found. Almost certainly, the presentation to the president closely followed the lines of McDonald's presentation to Wilbur on 28 February, stressing the strategic interests of the United States, especially should lands be found in the Polar Sea. Certainly McDonald also made the case that Amundsen's expedition would claim those lands for Norway should his expedition reach them first.

We do not know if Byrd's new plan was even discussed with the president. We do not know if the president was told specifically that the navy had no Loening Amphibians and that they would have to be obtained from the army. We do know that Coolidge promised to discuss the matter with his cabinet on Tuesday, 31 March (the same cabinet meeting that Byrd told Bartlett would determine if his Arctic expedition would be funded). Arrangements also were made for MacMillan to present a private lecture to the cabinet on the evening prior to the Tuesday cabinet meeting. As the group left the Oval Office, Congressman Britten turned and said to McDonald, "I think that you are going to get your planes for your expedition."

The next evening, MacMillan gave his lecture and then all awaited the results of the Tuesday cabinet meeting. The decision should not have been difficult on any level for either President Coolidge or his cabinet. In 1925, MacMillan was at the height of his fame and had spent more time in the Arctic than any other explorer; Byrd had no previous expedition experience. Coolidge admired entrepreneur industrialists, and McDonald was a swashbuckling entrepreneur Republican in the romantic new radio industry. Coolidge and his administration were Republicans; MacMillan was from Massachusetts and Maine and had the public support of Maine's powerful Republican Senator Frederick Hale, chairman of the Naval Affairs Committee, and of the influential Republican Congressman Britten; Byrd was a member of a Democratic dynasty from Virginia.

McDonald later related the cabinet meeting's outcome:

The next day I had a telephone call, requesting me to come to see the Secretary of the Navy, and Secretary Wilbur told me that I was going to get the planes we had requested. I complimented him on his vision and foresight, and he snapped back, "McDonald, you know just as well as I do that you got them from President Coolidge and not from me."

After the meeting, McDonald drafted and submitted a formal letter of understanding between the expedition and the navy.[11] Dated 4 April, the letter was signed by McDonald, who had MacMillan's power of attorney, and submitted to the secretary. This document, coupled with the 28 February letter from McDonald to Wilbur, form the complete agreement between the expedition and the navy. It is interesting to note McDonald's description of the expedition's command structure, located near the end of the April 4 agreement: "It is further understood, that under Donald B. MacMillan next in command shall be Lieutenant Commander R. E. Byrd, under whose supervision and direct charge shall come the Navy personnel and the Navy equipment assigned by the United States Navy Department."

It is not clear whether Byrd ever knew that McDonald's letter had listed Byrd as second in command of the entire expedition. As things would eventually work out, McDonald would hold that position, while Byrd would be in full command of the Naval Arctic Unit, the naval aviators attached to the expedition.

So, after a month-long campaign in Washington clearly led by McDonald, the 1925 MacMillan Arctic Expedition not only had the navy's approval, but, more importantly, the approval of President Coolidge along with his promise to equip the expedition with Loening Amphibians. McDonald stayed in Washington for the next ten days, developing the final plans for the expedition. Everyone was aware that they had less than ten weeks to select personnel, gather supplies, develop equipment, and set sail for the Far North. Both the navy and McDonald moved swiftly during the next week.

Byrd's reaction to the events was stated in a "strictly confidential" 10 April 1925 letter to his friend Fitzhugh Green:

Some time ago I had my own expedition underway and had raised the money from two of the wealthiest men in the world. This money had no strings on it. My plan was practically that which you have seen in the news-papers. Macmillan's plan was to go to the southern part of Greenland in the *Bowdoin,* which could probably not have gotten up to Etah this year: [*sic*] When he came to Washington I thought it was the ethical thing to tell him all about my plans, and did so.[12] The result of that was, it seemed to me, that he changed his plans so that they were practically the same as mine; went up to New York and chartered the steamer that Bartlett and I had intended to take with us, and asked for an additional plane. There might have been three planes available, but there were not four (I had asked for two); so it looked as if neither of us would go unless one of us was generous. I tried to do the gen-tlemanly thing and withdraw in case my insistence on my request would sink both of us. However, the Secretary, the Chief of Naval Operations, and the Assistant Secretary were very favorably inclined towards me, and I thought the best thing was for us to sort of combine.

When McDonald and I had a conference to combine, he insisted on rele-gating me completely to the background and taking away all rights and not even agreeing to my being second in command. In order to make harmony, I gave in on every point, but stated that I would have to take up the matter of being entirely tied up as to the aftermath in the matter of writing, talking, etc., with the Secretary of the Navy.

The Secretary and others protected me against my foolish self, and would not allow me to be tied up so that I can not give a talk in my own home if I want to.[13]

Now I have the impression quite strongly that I am up against an extremely selfish outfit that drive an extremely hard bargain. I am afraid I am going to be up against it, because McDonald does not seem to be able to give at all when a point arises, and I rather imagine McMillan [*sic*] is the same type. Now I am writing this in confidence to you as a friend, and I will appreciate it deeply your giving me any dope along this line that you can, so that I can know how to make my calculations. I appreciate your other letters deeply, and am looking forward to having a long talk with you about this matter.[14]

The National Geographic Society

On Monday, 6 April, the Navy Department issued a brief press release for the morning papers:

Following the assignment of naval aircraft and naval pilots for an aerial exploration of the arctic, the Navy Department announced today that the Expedition would be known as the "MacMillan Arctic Expedition, under the auspices of the National Geographic Society."

Dr. Gilbert Grosvenor, president of the National Geographic Society, today announced that the Society would contribute to the financing of the Expedition.

In a simultaneous six-page press release, the National Geographic Society detailed expedition plans. It gave the goal of the expedition as "the survey of the only remaining blind spot on the map of the world—a region of more than a million square miles in extent lying between Alaska and the North Pole" and the aerial survey of the interiors of Baffin and Ellesmere islands. The press release specifically stated that President Coolidge had endorsed the expedition with "respect to the assignment of Naval planes and aircraft" and announced that "Lt. Cdr. Byrd would have charge of all flight operations in connection with the expedition." The press release also detailed the radio experiments to be conducted:

The radio equipment of the expedition will be of special interest. In the words of E. F. McDonald of Chicago, who is giving particular attention to these details, "we will write radio history in the north this summer." Mr. McDonald is President of the Radio Broadcaster League [sic; McDonald was actually then the founding president of the National Association of Broadcasters] and is assembling the finest radio equipment procurable for the expedition. Sets for transmitting on 20, 40, 80 and 180 meters will be carried. With the 20 meter set Mr. McDonald expects to communicate with the outside world not only in code but also by voice. "It is altogether probable that people on the equator will hear the folk songs sung by the Eskimos in the Arctic this summer," said McDonald. Between the latitudes of 55 and 75 degrees there exists what has hitherto been an impenetrable band for radio communication. These latitudes also define the auroral band though it is not known whether any significance may be attached to this fact in connection with radio communication. The difficulties of daylight transmission and reception as compared with night broadcasting are well known to the radio fan. It may be recalled that there is no night during the summer months in

McDonald and MacMillan pose here in full uniform as lieutenant commanders, USNRF, during the planning of the 1925 expedition in May 1925.
Zenith

the Arctic, and this fact will be an additional handicap which will serve as a challenge to the expedition.

The radio operator for the expedition has not as yet been selected but a call for volunteers which will be issued in the near future is expected to turn up a host of radio enthusiasts as candidates for the post.

The Naval Arctic Unit

As soon as presidential approval for the expedition was received, Adm. W. A. Moffett, chief of the Bureau of Aeronautics, determined that the personnel for the Arctic Aviation Unit should be selected from volunteers, due to the potentially hazardous nature of flight in the Far North. A request for volunteers was issued to all navy and marine air stations and squadrons. In less

Side view of the Loening Amphibian, model OL-2. Aviation Pilot A. S. Nold, serving in the Naval Arctic Unit as a flight mechanic, is seen leaning against the hull, May 1925.
Schur Family and U.S. Navy

than one week, there were over sixty volunteer officers and men to fill eight slots. After some deliberation, Moffett selected Byrd; Lt. M. A. Schur and Chief Boatswain Earl E. Reber, USN, both highly respected flyers and former racing pilots; and five other noncommissioned naval personnel, including Floyd Bennett.

The full complement of the Naval Arctic Unit was:

Lt. Cdr. Richard. E. Byrd, USN (Ret.)

Lt. (j.g.) Cdr. M. A. Schur, USN[15]

Chief Boatswain E. E. Reber, USN (aviation pilot)[16]

Chief Machinist Mate, Aviation, Floyd Bennett, USN (aviation pilot)[17]

Chief Machinist Mate, Aviation, A. C. Nold, USN (aviation pilot)[18]

Lt. Cdr. Richard E. Byrd, USN (Ret.), at the Philadelphia Navy Yard in May 1925. One of the Loening Amphibians may be seen in the background.

Schur Family and U.S. Navy

Floyd Bennett, Lt. (j.g.) M. A. "Billie" Schur, and Chief Boatswain Earl E. Reber
pose at the Philadelphia Navy Yard during the preparation of the Loening
Amphibians, May 1925.
Schur Family and U.S. Navy

Chief Machinist Mate, Aviation, N. P. Sorensen, USN[19]

Aviation Machinist Mate 1st Class, C. F. Rocheville, USN[20]

Chief Aerographer Albert Francis, USN

The selected officers and men were ordered to report to the Bureau of
Aeronautics in Washington and then were assigned temporary duty with the
MacMillan Arctic Expedition. During the two months of preparation for
the expedition, Byrd worked out of the Bureau of Aeronautics at the Navy
Department, making frequent trips to the Navy Aircraft Factory at the Navy
Yard in Philadelphia where the Loening Amphibians were being prepared
for the expedition. Responsible for gathering the engineering supplies and
equipment for the trip, Lieutenant Schur also divided his time between the
bureau and the factory. Chief Boatswain Reber was assigned to the aircraft

factory, with liaison duties with the Loening aircraft plant in New York City. Chief Machinist Mate Sorensen was sent to the army's McCook Field "to familiarize himself with the peculiarities of the inverted Liberty engine." Chief Machinist Mates Nold and Bennett also were assigned to the Navy Aircraft Factory in Philadelphia. The entire Naval Arctic Unit was dedicated to an all-out effort to prepare the planes and all support equipment in less than sixty days for hazardous Arctic flight operations. Unfortunately, despite their almost superhuman efforts, events would prove that sixty days were simply not enough time to adequately prepare for a mission which sent an untried airframe and a radically reconfigured engine into the world's harshest flying environment.

Race to the Pole?

As plans for the MacMillan expedition matured, public interest in the expedition began to build rapidly, fed by press releases by all three sponsoring parties, the navy, the National Geographic Society, and Zenith Radio Corporation.

There were, in fact, two additional Arctic expeditions being planned for the spring and summer of 1925. The activities of all three groups were a constant source of news copy and rather sensational headlines. Some journals characterized the events of that spring and summer as "the most picturesque sporting event in the history of mankind with the possible exception of the aerial race around the world in 1924." A slightly less sensational headline led the front page of section nine of the Sunday *New York Times* of 26 April 1925:

THREE NATIONS IN AIR RACE FOR POLAR LAND
Uncharted Continent to Be Sought This Summer by America, Norway and Britain—MacMillan Has Support of U.S. Navy—Amundsen to Fly From Spitsbergen, Algarsson to Use Blimp

Three rival groups are speeding preparations to reach the North Pole by way of the air, to solve the secrets of The Top of The World and to bring back first, if they succeed in getting back, the solution of the Arctic mysteries that have always baffled science.

The first is the MacMillan–United States Navy Expedition. The second, headed by Roald Amundsen, using airplanes and starting in May, will carry the flag of Norway. Another, led by Grettir Algarsson of Liverpool, using a blimp, starting in mid-June, will bear the British flag.

Thus, with the American expedition starting in June, an international air race is in prospect. Aside from being the outstanding aeronautical event of the year, the competition promises to be the most thrilling—more spirited even than the round-the-world flight that the Americans won.

The long article went on to describe in detail the plans of each of the three expeditions. It stated that the race to a possible "lost continent" lying between Alaska and the Pole was the real goal. Today, it is not hard to visualize how the world strategic balance might have shifted had there, in fact, been a polar continent in that large area of unexplored territory and had explorers from one of the three countries claimed it for their nation. Prophetically, the article noted that many aeronautical experts considered Amundsen's plans, using two giant Dornier "Val" (Whale) monoplane seaplanes, "extremely risky" and suggested that the much more thoroughly planned MacMillan expedition, leaving a month later, might even have to become a rescue mission for the intrepid Amundsen.[21]

The Loening Amphibians

The airplanes that MacMillan and McDonald had been seeking since the beginning of the year were a type new to American aviation: amphibians. As MacMillan and McDonald were struggling to gain acceptance for their 1925 expedition plans, the brand-new Loening Amphibian seemed the perfect aircraft for exploring the Polar Sea. When they included it in their proposal to Secretary of the Navy Wilbur, they could not have imagined that they were also embroiling themselves and Grover Loening, the designer and manufacturer of the aircraft, in one of the most dramatic events in peacetime U.S. military history: the court-martial of visionary Army Air Service Gen. Billy Mitchell.

Though there had been at least marginally successful amphibian aircraft developed in Europe, an aircraft that was truly at home as a sea plane or land

The inverted engine of the Loening is seen here with the access panels removed, May 1925. The Liberty engine was inverted in the Loening to raise the crankshaft as high above the water as possible. This innovation apparently caused some difficulty on the expedition as each of the primary engines developed serious internal problems, probably related to inadequate oil supply. At the end of the expedition, all three spare engines had been used and at least one plane was inoperable due to engine trouble. The Loening Amphibian did, however, go on to give very reliable service with the army, navy, and marines.
Schur Family and U.S. Navy

plane awaited the entry of Grover Loening to the aviation scene. Loening was the first aeronautical engineering graduate from Columbia University and worked for some time as an assistant to Orville Wright. His small Manhattan-based aircraft company specialized in manufacturing small flying boats, including an innovative monoplane pusher-type "Flying Yacht" popular with wealthy sportsmen like Vincent Astor and Harold S. Vanderbilt. This aircraft had won the 1921 Collier Trophy. The assistant to the chief of the service, Gen. Billy Mitchell, acquired nine of the early Loening seaplanes so that the army would have rescue capability at seaside army airfields.

Single-engine pusher-type seaplanes had gained some acceptance in the years after World War I. However, they were often deadly to the pilot. In even a mild crackup, the momentum of the massive rear-facing engine, mounted directly behind the pilot, would carry it right through the cockpit. During early 1923, the Army Air Corps had developed an inverted version of the World War I Liberty aircraft engine in response to a direct order from General Mitchell. The purpose for inverting this water-cooled V-12 engine was to get the mass of the engine below the crankshaft and out of the pilot's line-of-sight forward. The one working version of this new engine configuration was introduced to the public at the 1923 St. Louis Air Races. Grover Loening attended the air races, examined the engine, and saw that this unusual engine configuration could be "the missing link" that would make possible the world's first tractor-type amphibian.

After several months of design work in New York, Loening submitted a rather brash "unsolicited proposal" for a new amphibian patrol craft to Chief of the Army Air Service Gen. Mason M. Patrick and his assistant, General Mitchell. Designed for safety and able to land in water or on snow, mud, or a normal runway, the Loening was an almost perfect aircraft for exploring rugged unknown territory or for patrolling coastal waters in most weather conditions. This latter point was particularly important to the Army Air Service. At that time, 1923–24, the AAS was locked in a territorial battle with the navy, each contending for the coastal patrol responsibilities in America's national defense plan.

After some consideration of Loening's proposal in Washington, General Mitchell called a meeting at Dayton's McCook Field to develop the army's response. General Mitchell did not support the idea and, according to Loening, intended to reject it. As Mitchell was en route, flying his own DH-4, his engine suddenly went dead over heavily wooded and mountainous country near the Ohio River. His only chance of survival was to ditch the plane in the swift-running river. The plane flipped over on impact, but somehow Mitchell got out and swam ashore. He walked to a telephone and called McCook Field, informing them emphatically, "I can't be at the conference, but I can give you my order now. Contract with Loening at once for his amphibian design."

The first prototype of the Loening Amphibian was flown from Long Island Sound in June 1924. After several successful flights, the prototype was destroyed while landing on the sound, clearly due to pilot error. In spite of this untimely accident, Generals Patrick and Mitchell authorized the construction of the ten Loening Amphibians in July 1924. The first of these ten amphibians was really a second "one-off" prototype and was designated as type COA-1 by Loening and as AS 24-8 by the army. It was first flown in January 1925 from Loening's East River plant to Bolling Field, Washington, D.C., for formal acceptance by the army.

The Loening's arrival in Washington was very timely; a record-breaking winter storm arrived soon after the Loening, grounding many aircraft due to the intense cold. One of the reasons to bring the Loening to Washington was to offer this innovative new design for the inspection of a "Select [Congressional] Committee on the Inquiry of the Air Services" recently formed to investigate several aviation scandals. While at Bolling Field, the Loening performed for the committee, several delegations of army and navy notables, and President Calvin Coolidge. The plane performed very well despite the frigid conditions, which continued to keep many conventional aircraft grounded. After the demonstration flights, the Air Service assigned the amphibian to McCook Field, Dayton for full engineering tests.

Unfortunately, the navy's first order for the new Loening Amphibians was placed quite some time after the initial army order. Delivery of the navy planes was not expected until early 1926. Available records do not explain exactly how the navy was able to persuade the army to loan the MacMillan expedition the precious Loenings. However, given the very contentious relationship between the two services in those years, and given the fact that army procurement of these unusual aircraft was due to the personal decision of General Mitchell, direct intervention by President Coolidge was almost surely necessary to wrest these new airplanes from the army. Whatever the case, the Naval Arctic Unit was authorized to accept the first two production models of the Loening Amphibian, each designated as Model OL-2, from the factory in New York City.

Shortwave Radio Communication

Since the inception of radio at the beginning of the twentieth century, commercial and military interests had focused on utilizing the lower frequency band that lies below the modern AM broadcasting band. These frequencies are called "longwave" radio. Longwave stations required large electric motor-like alternators, some taller than a man, to generate the power required to send signals reliably over long distances. The navies of the world adopted longwave for both ship-to-ship and ship-to-shore communications. However, the bulk of the massive longwave transmitters limited the use of radio to shore stations and a few of the largest combat vessels. Unfortunately, physical characteristics of the ionosphere limited long-distance longwave radio communication exclusively to nighttime use. This nighttime-only restriction, coupled with the bulk and cost of longwave transmitters, severely limited the usefulness of radio, especially in the fleet. As longwave radio frequencies became overcrowded, the numerous transmissions between amateur radio operators began to seriously interfere with commercial and military transmissions. Just prior to World War I, amateur radio operations were relegated to the spectra that we know today as "medium wave" and "shortwave" radio. At that time, these two bands were thought to be useless for anything more than regional communications.

As amateur radio reemerged after World War I, "hams" utilized new technology developed during the war and quickly achieved startling results with their lightweight, relatively inexpensive shortwave gear. Rather quickly, hams were relaying messages from coast to coast. In 1922, the signals of American hams were heard in Europe. In 1923, distance records for reception and, more importantly, two-way communications fell almost monthly. In the spring of 1923, signals from American hams were heard in both Australia and New Zealand. Most significantly, early in the morning of 27 November 1923, leading American amateur operators Fred Schnell, operating station 1MO, and John Reinartz, station 1ZAM, established two-way transatlantic communication with the French amateur station, F8AB, operated by Leon Deloy in Nice. This long-awaited but still startling accomplishment was achieved with equipment—shortwave equipment—which was orders of magnitude less expensive and less bulky than that required for longwave transmissions. Further, the radio amateurs soon demonstrated that shortwave frequencies could support communications over global distances twenty-four hours a day! The rapidity of change in radio technology in the early 1920s and the implications on society were probably as profound and swift as those of the PC revolution in the 1990s.[22] Zenith's McDonald was intensely aware of these developments and quite concerned that the navy was not moving quickly enough to adopt this new technology.

The U.S. Navy and Shortwave

The needs of fleet communications and emergent naval aviation mandated close attention by the navy to developments in radio communication. In fact, capital ships of the U.S. fleet had carried very bulky longwave equipment since just before America's entry into World War I. The navy had been experimenting with higher frequencies since 1921 and had begun to study propagation in the shortwave spectrum shortly thereafter. The head of the Naval Radio Laboratory noted in later years that the bridging of the Atlantic by American and French amateurs operating on one hundred meters (November 1923) was the beginning of serious naval interest in these shorter wavelengths. As transatlantic communication by amateurs became more routine in 1923–24, and as the phenomenon of shortwave signals "skipping" off the underside of the ionosphere became understood, research at the Naval Radio Laboratory struggled to keep pace with the amateur community. Hoyt Taylor, superintendent, Radio Division, U.S. Naval Research Laboratory, urged the placement of high-frequency radio equipment on the *Shenandoah* at its completion in early 1924. Although the *Shenandoah* did not make its planned polar flight in the summer of 1924, very good results were obtained with the new radio equipment during a shakedown cruise across the United States in October 1924. Radio signals were heard and copied forty-two hundred miles away, while the conventional longwave transmissions were ineffective.[23] The new equipment operated at frequencies that fall just within the lower edge of the shortwave spectrum. Most importantly, although these new frequencies could support long-distance communications at night, like longwave, the *Shenandoah*'s new equipment could not communicate over long distances during daylight hours. The commander in chief, U.S. Fleet, was not impressed with the results of the *Shenandoah* radio experiments and insisted that dirigibles continue to operate on "standard frequencies" (longwave). Throughout the fleet, as well, the navy continued to depend on the now traditional, bulky transmitters, which operated in the longwave (low-frequency) spectrum.

McDonald's Influence

McDonald also took his role as a reserve officer in naval intelligence very seriously. A personal two-page memo to McDonald from Staff Headquarters, Ninth Naval District, discussed the desire of the chief of naval operations to enroll "several thousand of these amateurs as radio operators in Class 6 of the Naval Reserve Force," and went on to detail use of the seventy-six-meter (true shortwave) transmitter at Great Lakes Naval Training Station. The purpose of this transmitter would be to train operators in the Ninth District in proper naval communications procedures. There are indications in the Zenith archives that Commander McDonald played an important role in the adoption of shortwave communication at the fleet level. After all, the founders of Zenith—McDonald, Mathews, and Hassel—were all former navy men, and both McDonald and Mathews were very active in the navy reserve.

Only fragments of McDonald's 1924 correspondence with the navy have survived. In February of that year, he wrote directly to Capt. O. P. Jackson, then director of naval communications, about developments in amateur radio and the potential usefulness of the ARRL as an organization to harness the amateurs in support of naval developments in communications. He received a decidedly negative and bureaucratic response.

In later years, McDonald related that, in 1924 and 1925, he was deeply concerned that the hidebound upper echelons of the navy, deeply committed to longwave communication, would ignore the new developments on shortwave. Incidents on the 1925 expedition would show that McDonald's concerns were well-founded.

Capt. Ridley McLean replaced Captain Jackson as the director, naval communications, in July 1924. McLean's decision to authorize shortwave radio communications experiments involving the U.S. Battle Fleet during a tour of Australia and New Zealand in the summer of 1925 is an important pivot point in the history of long-distance communications. In Howeth's monumental work, *History of Communications: Electronics in the United States Navy*, he relates that McLean became interested in the potential benefits of the shortwave frequencies after the fall 1924 *Shenandoah* flight. Howeth gives no details of just why McLean determined that the fleet's summer 1925 cruise would provide an excellent opportunity to test high-frequency radio use by the fleet. Howeth also fails to record McLean's reasons for inducting a radio amateur into the navy to conduct these experiments and placing him aboard the command vessel of the 1925 summer cruise, the USS *Seattle*.

The fragmentary McDonald files for 1925 do not contain the bulk of correspondence between McDonald and the navy. However, circumstantial evidence published in *QST* magazine in 1925 and the Zenith corporate history, published prior to McDonald's death in the 1950s, describe McDonald's personal role in convincing Captain McLean to undertake the fleet shortwave communications experiments in the summer of 1925. Both sources indicate that McDonald was personally responsible for ARRL Traffic Manager Fred Schnell's being commissioned a navy lieutenant and being placed aboard the USS *Seattle* for the Pacific cruise of 1925. The *Seattle* was the flagship of Adm. R. E. Coontz, commander in chief of the U.S. Fleet. In addition to the USS *Seattle*, that spring and summer the fleet had another amateur station, 6TS, operated by Ed Willis, aboard the USS *Relief* operating as navy station NEPQ. The fleet sailed from San Francisco on 14 April 1925. The shortwave experiments of that summer, by the navy and between the MacMillan expedition and the fleet, would change the history of long-distance communication forever.

Radio Equipment for the Expedition

With shortwave equipment and techniques in their infancy, and with short-wave avionics totally unknown in 1925, Zenith engineers were hard-pressed to develop the expedition equipment in less than two months—mid-April to mid-June, 1925. To assist the effort, McDonald reached into the ranks of amateur radio operators and hired John L. Reinartz, recognized as a self-taught but brilliant young circuit designer and radio propagation theoretician. Reinartz, the other American amateur involved in the first transatlantic contact along with Fred Schnell, was hired to assist the amateur community as they explored these new truly "short" waves. A Zenith press release that spring reported his salary as $1,000 per month, "the highest salary ever paid to a radio operator."

One of Reinartz's main responsibilities was offering encouragement to his fellow amateurs to migrate from their former area of operations, now shared with AM broadcasters, to the new shortwave bands. The initial expedition-related Zenith press release noted that "during the last MacMillan Expedition [1923–24] there were 17,000 American amateurs who could receive and transmit on 180 meters (medium wave), and that now [spring 1925] there were only 20 American amateurs who could do so on short-wave."

Soon thereafter, Zenith distributed another release that described in complete detail how to construct a "Reinartz-Zenith Shortwave Receiver" and a similarly named transmitter. Assistance to the amateur community continued after the return of the expedition, when Zenith published a second set of plans for constructing a more advanced shortwave receiver and transmitter. Karl Hassel signed the November 1925 cover letter that accompanied these plans. The letter spoke of Zenith's desire to share its knowledge with the amateur community; the letter also expressed Zenith's lack of commercial interests in shortwave.

April and May of 1925 were frantic times for the Zenith engineers responsible for the expedition's radio equipment. Karl Hassel led the design team, with Zenith's chief engineer, H. C. Forbes, and John Reinartz also

The special-built Zenith shortwave transmitter as installed on the *Bowdoin* in May 1925.
Zenith

making major contributions. The shortwave transmitters were 250-watt and 2-kilowatt units (aboard the *Bowdoin* and *Peary* respectively) capable of transmitting on 20, 40, 80, and 275 meters. (In fact, most long-distance communication on the expedition took place on 40 meters.) It is important to note that the transmitting equipment aboard the *Bowdoin* was assembled and tested in Chicago before it was sent to Wiscasset, Maine, for installation, but that the transmitter aboard the second ship of the expedition, the *Peary*, was not. The size and configuration of the radio room aboard the *Peary* was not known until late in the spring, due to the time it took to locate and purchase the ship. As a result, the *Peary*'s much more powerful transmitter was not assembled and thoroughly tested in Chicago, as the *Bowdoin*'s equipment had been. Among the receivers taken along was the Reinartz-Zenith receiver, a Super Zenith broadcast receiver, a longwave receiver for press messages and time signals, and two portable loop broadcasting receivers for use by exploring parties or planes in distress.

John Reinartz was primarily responsible for the design of the innovative shortwave transceiver that the Loening Amphibians would use. A prototype of the transceiver was placed aboard a seaplane and tested extensively in mid-May with flights over, and landings on, Lake Michigan. A Zenith press release during those tests relates that this "Reinartz-Zenith" set was the first aircraft set able to operate whether or not the plane was flying. Apparently, all previous aircraft sets had been powered by wind-driven generators, usually mounted on the wing. The Reinartz design operated exclusively on batteries. This was extremely important, since wind generators driven by the aircraft's slipstream would have been useless to power emergency communication had these new type of aircraft been forced down in the Arctic.

The Peary

The expedition also required a second vessel, much larger than MacMillan's schooner *Bowdoin,* to transport aircraft, supplies, and personnel. Initially, the 1884-built Dundee whaler *Thetis* was identified as the second vessel for the expedition. She was a well-known Arctic vessel that had taken part in the Greely relief expedition. When it was determined that the *Thetis* was too small, McDonald—who was apparently in charge of this part of the planning, too—planned to use the *Neptune,* the vessel that had retrieved MacMillan and his men at the close of the Crocker Land Expedition in 1917. In early May, after delaying two weeks, the army agreed to supply a third Loening Amphibian for the expedition. The *Neptune*'s deck proved too small to accommodate three aircraft, so yet a third ship was sought to serve as the mothership for the amphibians. Evidence suggests that Zenith's McDonald, rather than MacMillan, as has been previously reported, purchased the third vessel for the expedition from his own pocket. She was a converted French minesweeper, then fitted out as a large steam-powered yacht called the *Rowena,* and was built along the lines of a fishing trawler, with very powerful engines and a massive nine-foot-diameter propeller. In a very short time, the *Rowena* was partially refitted at the Brooklyn Navy Yard and christened on 19 May 1925 as the ss *Peary*, named by MacMillan to honor his former commander.

The *Peary* was christened by Rear Admiral Peary's daughter, Marie Peary Stafford, called the "snow baby" by the press because she was born at one of her father's far northern headquarters. Navy airplanes circled during the ceremony, and navy and National Geographic Society officials were in attendance.

Back at the Philadelphia Navy Yard

At the beginning of May, plans and preparations for the aircraft were proceeding at a hectic pace. By mid-May, Lieutenant Schur and Chief Boatswain Reber were authorized to proceed to New York City to take delivery of the first two Loening Amphibians. On 15 May, at 4:00 P.M., the two Loenings were launched into the East River and christened NA-1 and NA-2 (the "NA" stood for Naval Arctic). Schur and Reber then took off and proceeded the short distance to Mitchell Field. They lowered the landing gear and set down at Mitchell for the night. The next day, they posed with the planes for the numerous news photographers and then took off for the Naval Aircraft Factory in Philadelphia.

One incident at the aircraft factory gives some insight into Lieutenant Commander Byrd's early grasp of the importance of media exposure and his somewhat difficult relationship with some of the men who served under him. When he journeyed to Philadelphia to inspect the first two Loenings, he was accompanied by a navy photographer detailed to take personal shots of Byrd with the aircraft and also, apparently, by a movie news photographer from Pathé News. While Byrd's consciousness of the public relations dimension of the expedition served both the navy and his own purposes very well, it did little to endear him to the men of the Naval Arctic Unit who were then working eighteen-hour days preparing for the expedition.

At the Naval Aircraft Factory, the next four weeks were a blur. Planes were modified for long-range Arctic service, and engine and airframe spares were collected. In addition, the expedition purchased lightweight camping and survival gear, concentrated food, Arctic clothing, and medical gear. Reber paused long enough to return to New York to accept the third Loening (NA-3) and fly her back to Philadelphia. Schur wrote later that it was a pleasure to see how fast all the paperwork was handled when the chips were down. He also noted that just about everyone was working night shifts. Radio tests were performed with the new shortwave gear and specialized navigation equipment (such as earth induction compasses and special drift indicators) was installed. At some point in that very busy time, the departure date was moved slightly ahead so that the farewell ceremonies planned for Boston would coincide with the celebration of the 150th anniversary of the Battle of Bunker Hill. Preparation work on the Loenings ceased at the Philadelphia Navy Yard at 2:00 A.M. on 10 June.

The Final Frantic Days

In the first few days of June, a Zenith team led by John Reinartz installed the radio equipment aboard the *Bowdoin* at her berth in Maine. John Reinartz and possibly some of the Zenith engineers also spent considerably more time at Boston Navy Yard, where they assembled the much more powerful transmitter on board the *Peary*. As McDonald and the *Peary* radio operators Paul McGee and Harold Gray would learn, the design and construction of the *Peary* transmitter was not complete as the expedition prepared to depart.

At 2:30 P.M. on 10 June, the three Loenings taxied down the ramp at the Naval Aircraft Factory in Philadelphia into the Delaware River and took off for Squantum Naval Reserve Air Station near Boston. Chief Boatswain E. E. Reber piloted NA-1 with Lieutenant Commander Byrd as navigator; Lt. M. A. Schur piloted NA-2 with AMM 1/c Rocheville aboard as mechanic, and Chief Machinist Mate Floyd Bennett flew NA-3 with ACCM A. C. Nold aboard. NA-3 became separated from the other two planes over New Jersey. About forty miles from Montauk Point, NA-1 and NA-2 ran into heavy fog and, after a great deal of course maneuvering, managed to land at Squan-

The Loening Amphibians were dismantled at the Boston Navy Yard and placed on board the *Peary* for the trip north. Here, seamen carry one of the wing sets down the dock to be further dismantled and stowed in crates aboard the *Peary*. The three partially dismantled Loenings may be seen in the left, center, and right background (16 June 1925).
Zenith

tum at 5:00 P.M. NA-3 reached Squantum the following morning at 8:00 A.M. after being grounded by the fog and spending the night on the beach at the northern end of Cape Cod Canal.

For the next three days, radio test hops were made at Naval Reserve Air Station, Squantum, with the Loenings operating as seaplanes. Modifications of the new planes continued: a 13 June 1925 letter from the Naval Aircraft Factory, for example, contained a hand-drawn sketch of a modification to the reserve oil tanks that had not been finished at the factory in Philadelphia. On 14 June the planes proceeded to Boston Airport, landing as land planes. At the Boston airport, various final adjustments and instrument

Lieutenant Schur's NA-2 is already secured in its special cradle on the afterdeck of the *Peary*. A floating crane is lifting the second fuselage aboard. Note the large crate amidships (lower right), which contains wings already stowed aboard (16 June 1925).
Schur Family and U.S. Navy

calibrations (compass deviations) were performed, and on Monday, 15 June, all three planes were flown to the Navy Yard where they were hoisted up to the dock alongside the *Peary* by a large floating crane. In thirty-six frantic hours, the wing sets were removed, dismantled, and stowed in large wooden crates (which were lashed amidships on either side of the superstructure of the *Peary*). The floating crane was then used to lift each fuselage into specially constructed afterdeck cradles. In his official activities report, Byrd was particularly appreciative of the support and effort put forth by the Navy Yard personnel during those very busy hours. Thanks to everyone's efforts, as dawn approached on 17 June, the planes and gear were aboard and secure and the public departure ceremonies could begin on time.

Boston's Farewell Celebration

The ss *Peary* sailed from Charleston Navy Yard, Boston, on 17 June 1925. Lt. Cdr. E. F. McDonald Jr. was in command, with George F. Steele of Roxbury, Massachusetts, as captain of the vessel. The National Geographic Society was represented aboard the *Peary* by Jacob Gayer, staff photographer, and by Prof. William N. Koelz, an ichthyologist.

Looking back across almost three-quarters of a century of exploration and conspicuous bravery—from Lindbergh's flight to the lunar landings and beyond—it is hard for us to realize how important this expedition was and in what high regard its members were held by the general public. The departure from Boston was a public event of national importance, attended by thousands of well-wishers and heavily covered in the press. This festive occasion was best described in the unpublished journal of Lieutenant Schur:

> Speeches were made beginning at 11:00 A.M. from the deck of the uss *Constitution* by Gov. Fuller of Mass, Mayor Hurley [actually, Curley] of Boston and Donald MacMillan. Dr. MacMillan's speech called attention to the Navy flyers on board the *Peary* across the dock from the famous *Constitution,* all eyes were turned toward us, who were lined up on the *Peary*'s bridge. It was a thrilling moment; we all realized we were to follow an able explorer.
>
> The Ass't. Sec. [of the] Navy, Mr. Robinson personally came over on the *Peary* to meet us. I certainly was impressed by his spirit of cheerfulness and his hearty handshake. Several thousand people stood on the dock to cheer us off, really they thought we were on a perilous mission, to me it seemed as though I was only going on a short cross country flight, all the Navy men in the expedition [*sic*] faces were drawn, and they looked tired.
>
> Promptly at twelve, lines were cast off and the *Peary* steamed out, headed for Wiscasset, Maine, what a thrilling moment for me, really I can hardly express my emotion, I could see her hitting the ice field already. I would not miss this trip for anything, but now my mind runs back to home, my dear wife, she certainly has given up a lot, so I could go on this trip, God bless her.

The *Peary* must have been quite a sight as she weighed anchor and steamed down the Charles River with three large Loening OL-2 Amphibians secured

The combined celebration of the 150th anniversary of Bunker Hill and the departure ceremonies for the ss *Peary* occurred on 17 June 1925, with thousands of well-wishers in attendance. The culmination of the daylong ceremonies took place aboard and alongside the historic USS *Constitution*. The *Peary* was docked parallel to the *Constitution* with the crowd between the two ships. Governor Fuller of Massachusetts, Mayor Curley of Boston, and Lieutenant Commander MacMillan were among the dignitaries who addressed the crowd.
Schur Family and U.S. Navy

to her afterdeck. She was escorted down river by several steam launches, a Boston Harbor fireboat spraying celebratory water plumes, and two Navy Eagle patrol boats, which were to escort her to Wiscasset.

Farewell Celebrations at Wiscasset

The *Peary* joined the *Bowdoin* in Wiscasset, Maine, early on the eighteenth and all hands spent the next two days loading supplies. U. J. "Sport" Herrmann, Commander McDonald's lifelong friend, became the first casualty of the expedition when he "put one Liberty [aircraft engine] aboard alone" and badly jammed a finger in the process. The injury was serious enough to require surgery when the expedition reached Battle Harbor, Labrador.

The *Peary* contingent of the 1925 MacMillan Arctic Expedition, June 1925.
Standing (left to right) in back row: Hosmer L. Freeman, mate; Capt. George F.
Steele; Lieutenant Commander McDonald; an unidentified chief engineer;
Lieutenant Commander MacMillan; unidentified; Henry Forbes, engineer;
unidentified; Paul McGee, chief operator; Herman Meinhart, engineer; Cdr.
U. J. "Sport" Herrmann; and unidentified.
 Front row (left to right): Charles F. Rocheville, AMM 1/c, USN; Lieutenant (j.g.)
Schur; Chief Boatswain Reber, USN; "Sport" Herrmann's dog, Rowdy; and
Harold Gray, second radio operator. The last three men are unidentified.
Not shown: Lieutenant Commander Byrd.
Zenith

On the twentieth, the day the expedition sailed from Wiscasset, it seemed
to McDonald that "every native of Maine," as well as the faculty of Bowdoin
College and the governor of the state had traveled to Wiscasset to see them
off. Even though written descriptions of this event were found in both the
MacMillan and McDonald papers, again, it is the journal of navy flyer Lt. M.
A. Schur that gives us the best sense of this tumultuous sendoff:

Dockside at Wiscasset, just moments before the expedition sails, 20 June 1925. The *Bowdoin* is in the foreground. The *Peary* with the Loenings on the afterdeck is standing out from the dock (center).
Zenith

It is now ten A.M. The crowds are beginning to line up on the dock. Army sentries are roping off passageways for our friends and officials. All the vendors are crying out, trying to sell all the ice cream, popcorn, candy, etc. If they fail to dispose of it today, they never could sell it in Wiscasset in months. We are asked to pose for the numerous cameras and Kodaks, people are wishing us good bye, really I hope they don't think we are never going to return.

It is near one o'clock, we are to leave at two; the governor [Brewster] of Maine wishes us to walk to the little church at Wiscasset with him, where the town has made preparations for our farewell; we follow the band; people on every side are waving and cheering us; Reber and I are marching side by side, rear of Major General Greely the famous old explorer; we at last arrive at the church after climbing some of Maine's famous rocky hills. After the Governor had seated himself, the Navy took over the top step of the church, immediately the citizens of Maine, as they were referred to in all the speeches, took possession of the vacant steps. While the Governor was explaining the mission of the gathering there was a crash, the church steps caved in, on all sides people laughed, to me it seemed as tho the governor's platform fell through.

Following a round of speeches, Reber and I hiked back to the ship, only to find she was at anchor in the stream, so we boarded the *Bowdoin,* I helped MacMillan at the wheel and we now cast off all lines and steamed down near the *Peary,* circling up again past the dock, thousands of people waving and cheering us God speed, whereupon the *Bowdoin* was brought along side the *Peary,* like the Navy of old, we jumped the *Peary*'s rail and swung ourselves on board. The *Peary* hauled up her anchor and down the river we steamed followed by the *Bowdoin* and several small boats. At times we had to slow down to allow the *Bowdoin* to catch up, also the two Navy Eagle Boats had to slow down for the *Peary,* really it was a parade.

The youngest member of the expedition was a fourteen-year-old Chicago native, Kennett Rawson, who was serving as an able-bodied seaman aboard the *Bowdoin.* Soon after returning from the expedition, he published this account of the expedition's sailing in his book, *A Boy's Eye View of the Arctic:*

Eager hands freed the lines [of the *Bowdoin*] and amid the roar of steam whistles and cheers from the crowd, we slowly steamed seaward. Governor Brewster of Maine had furnished a band and a tug to transport them, and as we steamed outward they poured forth a brazen blare of melody. Alumni and students of [nearby] Bowdoin College, the Commander's [MacMillan] alma mater had chartered a steamer, and the enthusiastic, leather-lunged collegians raked us fore and aft with a series of vocal salvos that would have driven any team on to victory. The procession was headed by two naval vessels especially designated by the Navy Department to do honor to the occasion. In addition to this official recognition, a large number of yachts from far and near had gathered to join in the celebration. But as we reeled off the miles, our escorts gradually turned back one by one, until by the time we neared the open sea, only a persistent few remained.

THREE

The Expedition Sails North

*T*HE 1925 MacMillan Arctic Expedition offi-
cially set sail as scheduled, at 2:00 P.M., 20 June 1925. After sailing the last few
miles down the Sheepscot River, taking on water in Boothbay Harbor
(*Peary*) and offloading the final well-wishers on Monhegan Island (*Bowdoin*), the two vessels turned hard aport and made for Sydney, Cape Breton
Island via Cape Sable, Nova Scotia. Fog over most of the route was so thick
that little of the coast or normal navigational references were seen. Nevertheless, the faster *Peary* arrived at Sydney at 5:00 P.M. on 23 June. The *Bowdoin* sailed into the North Sydney harbor at noon the next day.

Throughout early June, extensive communications plans had been
developed jointly by MacMillan, Zenith, and the navy. Letters and memos
in the files of both MacMillan and McDonald record Navy Secretary
Wilbur's close personal involvement in these plans. Even so, there was still
one major "misunderstanding" between the expedition and Wilbur that very
nearly scuttled the entire undertaking as the ships sailed north up the coast.
Wilbur wanted the *Peary* to be equipped with a large longwave transmitter

formerly installed on the battleship USS *Florida*. Wilbur was not a radioman, but he was aware of the navy's considerable reliance on longwave equipment. He wished such equipment aboard to "insure the safety of the men and planes," even though the longwave transmitter was very large and heavy and would have limited range in the constant daylight of the North. The large *Florida* longwave transmitter was in addition to a "high power low frequency tube transmitter using one kilowatt Navy vacuum tubes" that was required by the Navy Bureau of Engineering.

MacMillan and McDonald agreed to Secretary Wilbur's request; however, the *Peary* had sailed from Wiscasset without the *Florida*'s transmitter aboard. For some time, Secretary Wilbur thought that the transmitter had been left behind intentionally. He sent a strong radiogram to MacMillan who, by that time, was at sea on the way to Sydney. MacMillan immediately responded that the expedition indeed *wanted* the navy radio aboard and suggested that *Florida*'s radio be sent north to Sydney, where they would wait as long as necessary for its arrival. Byrd wired Wilbur: "Understand that news despatch stated that expedition refused to take Florida set aboard. That is not the case. This occurrence is due to a misunderstanding."

Byrd explained the incident to Secretary Wilbur after the expedition:

> There was no friction between Commander MacMillan and the personnel of the Navy attached to the MacMillan Arctic Expedition before, during, or after the Expedition. The types of radio to be used were decided at two conferences held on the second and fourth of May. Commander MacMillan was present at one of these conferences, and his representative, E. F. MacDonald [*sic*], was present at both of them. An understanding was reached at these conferences as to what radio would be carried, and there was no friction or disagreement about the understanding. It was agreed that the Navy spark set which was taken from the battleship *Florida* was to be put on the *Bowdoin*. This spark set was sent to Wiscasset, Maine, as the *Bowdoin* was there.
>
> However, it was found that the *Bowdoin* was so deeply laden with supplies that there was no room for the spark set, nor was there room for the set on the *Peary*, which was also deeply laden and deep in the water. On June the 19th a dispatch was sent to me from the Navy Department directed to the *Bowdoin*, and this was received by Lieutenant Commander E. F. MacDonald

[*sic*], Naval Reserve Officer. As I was absent at a dinner given to the expedition, and as my return that night was doubtful, MacDonald [sic] answered the telegram. His telegram read in part as follows: "It was agreed that *Florida* 'five kilowatt' spark set was to be installed *Bowdoin* and for the purpose shipped to Wiscasset. Every available foot of space is occupied on *Bowdoin* and *Peary* absolutely impossible to take *Florida* set aboard." Then he went on to say "Can remove two or three of our spare Liberty airplane motors from deck of *Bowdoin* and replace with spark set if you so order." Next morning when I was informed about these dispatches I sent a dispatch to the Department stating that I would rather not leave behind any Liberty motors and asked for advice from the department as to what to do. I then waited at the telegraph office for an answer to my dispatch.

We sailed that day at two P.M., and I later found out that my dispatch had not reached the Department until after two P.M., and we therefore had to sail without putting the *Florida* set on board, and it was not a matter of disagreement between Commander MacMillan and myself but was a matter of loading. The *Florida* spark set is a very large set, and would take up a great deal of space. The *Bowdoin* is only about eighty feet long and the *Peary* only about one hundred and thirty-four feet long with a displacement of about three hundred and fifty tons. The Navy then decided that it was more important to have the spark set on board than some of the equipment, and therefore sent the set up to Sydney by the destroyer *Putnam*. Commander MacMillan agreed immediately to put the set on board the *Peary* as it was impracticable to get it on the *Bowdoin*. Commander MacMillan had no objection whatever to taking the type of sets the Navy Department wanted him to take.

Secretary Wilbur sent Byrd a final radiogram on the subject that clarified the official navy position for all concerned:

Sch Bowdoin 0022 Lt. Com. R. E. Byrd Florida spark set is being sent you at Sydney by Destroyer Putnam period planes will not repeat not take flight away from vicinity of base until spark set is installed to insure communications with planes and to give compass bearings to planes as originally agreed upon period inform MacMillan of departments decision which is for purposes of safe guarding planes and personnel period if these instructions cannot be complied with arrange to land planes and personnel at Sydney for return to United States.

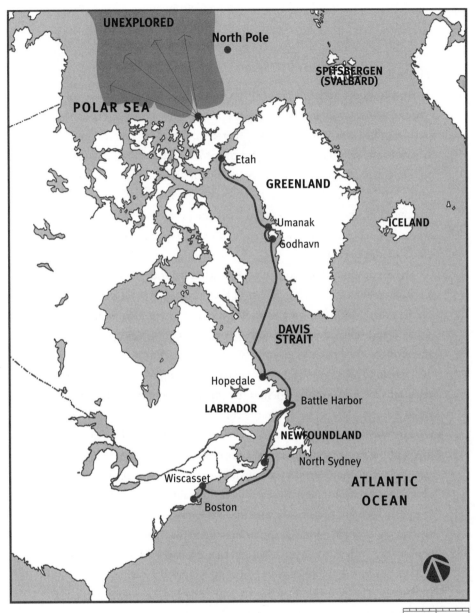

UNEXPLORED

North Pole

SPITSBERGEN
(SVALBARD)

POLAR SEA

Etah

GREENLAND

ICELAND

Umanak

Godhavn

DAVIS
STRAIT

Hopedale

Battle Harbor

LABRADOR

NEWFOUNDLAND

North Sydney

Wiscasset

ATLANTIC
OCEAN

Boston

0   250   500
miles

THE EXPEDITION SAILS NORTH
John H. Bryant, FAIA

The fast navy destroyer *Putnam* arrived in North Sydney on 25 June and the *Peary* took the longwave transmitter aboard. This entire incident later became a matter of contention during the court-martial trial of Col. Billy Mitchell.

An additional problem plagued the *Peary* almost from the time she left Wiscasset. McDonald had ordered two 2,000-volt generators and had instead been supplied with two 1,000-volt generators. During the early days of the trip north he sent many cables about the problem to the manufacturer and to others who might be of help. The generator armatures burned out after only a few hours' use and the problem was compounded when the radio was in operation. Two weeks into the journey the problem with the generators was solved when the *Peary*'s radio operators, McGee and Gray, rewired the *Peary*'s radio system.

The expedition lay in North Sydney harbor for four days taking aboard fresh provisions and having $^7/_{16}$" steel plates bolted over all hull portholes on the *Peary*. McDonald's log notes that the crew voted unanimously to give up light and ventilation below decks in order to attach these plates as additional protection from damage by ice floes. The stop in Sydney allowed McDonald to take care of a flurry of personal communication; in one of his telegrams, he told Zenith's Roemer that the radio equipment was "making radio history" and that he was "more confident each day that we will put the voice of the Eskimo back to civilization." McDonald, Sport Herrmann, and a few of the others were "the toast of Sydney," being entertained royally at the yacht club one evening and inviting several Canadian army officers aboard for a send-off party the evening before sailing. McDonald notes that the party lasted until 3:00 A.M. and that the expedition weighed anchor on time at 5:30 A.M.! McDonald's log also recorded that there were sixty tons of coal aboard (thirty stored on deck) and that the *Peary* was so heavily loaded that the forecastle portholes were constantly underwater when the ship was under way. The expedition left North Sydney harbor bound for Battle Harbor, Labrador, early on the morning of 28 June 1925.

Battle Harbor

Very thick fog closed in as soon as the expedition cleared North Sydney harbor. The two ships proceeded independently, feeling their way across sixty-mile-wide Cabot Strait and finding the west coast of Newfoundland Island. They proceeded slowly north along the Newfoundland coast through intermittent dense fog. McDonald's reports to the National Geographic Society describe waters thick with Newfoundlanders in one-man dories fishing for cod. He was most eloquent, though, when describing the grinding poverty evident in the scattered fishing villages on this remote coast. Though there was some clear sailing, the fog was so thick at times that they simply hove to for long periods. About a third of the way up the coast, the weather cleared and the *Peary* again made very good time. She continued north up the west coast of Newfoundland, almost to the Strait of Belle Isle, before crossing to the southern coast of Labrador.

Both ships made landfall at Point Amour, near the modern-day Quebec-Labrador border. Independently, each paused nearby at one of the most startling sights on the Labrador coast, the wreck of the Royal Navy cruiser HMS *Raleigh*. Some years before, the *Raleigh* had run fatally aground and had since laid perfectly upright but fast on the rocks parallel to the shore, to all appearances still under way.

As the *Peary* reached the area, the weather deteriorated rapidly—a "blow" —and the ship dropped anchor to wait out the storm. At 6:00 P.M. Commander McDonald, Sport Herrmann, and Lieutenant Schur decided to take one of the *Peary*'s dories and row over to inspect the wreck. Schur noted that the wind was thirty knots, the sea quite choppy, and that they "gave the rest of the boys a thrill by even suggesting the trip." They made the trip without incident, even boarding the *Raleigh*. They found that the local fishermen had picked the cruiser so clean that they could not find even small souvenirs. They each remarked later in their journals how sad it was to see such a great man-of-war being pounded to pieces by the sea and the ice.

The wind dropped at 2:00 A.M., and the *Peary* proceeded through intermittent fog and occasional icebergs up the Labrador coast past Red Bay. The ship met MacMillan and the *Bowdoin* outside Battle Harbor, the unofficial capital of the Labrador coast, and dropped anchor in the harbor there at 1:00 P.M. on 2 July.

The stop at Battle Harbor was made primarily to purchase a few necessities and to put ashore the last passengers not headed for the Far North: Gilbert Grosvenor, president of the National Geographic Society; Sport Herrmann; and Dr. Wilfred Grenfell, an American medical missionary. Dr. Grenfell's headquarters and hospital, staffed by a few American nurses, was at Battle Harbor.

The brief stop stretched into several days as the expedition waited for clearer weather and for the ice pack to break up. Lieutenant Commander MacMillan had become increasingly concerned about ice conditions along the northern two-thirds of the Labrador coast. In normal years, this coastal ice pack broke up in early June. Explaining why the ice had not yet broken, elderly local fishermen reported that the spring of 1925 was the coldest in memory.

The time in Battle Harbor was not wasted. In addition to work on the equipment and the aircraft, a party was held for the nurses at Grenfell's hospital, and several groups went on local fishing expeditions. Aboard the *Peary*, the evening of 3 July was spent in a farewell party for Sport Herrmann and his dog "Rowdy." Sport had proven to be one of the most popular and hardworking members of the crew and would be "sorely missed." As midnight and the American Independence Day approached on that rather liquid evening, McDonald, Herrmann, Schur, and most of the *Peary*'s complement decided to celebrate the advent of July fourth with a fusillade of gunfire. They broke out every gun on board; McDonald's General George Armstrong Custer's revolver, .45-caliber service automatics, Winchester and Springfield rifles, shotguns, and even flare pistols were put to use with great gusto at exactly midnight. They expected their salutes to be returned by the crew of the *Bowdoin*, but it had turned in hours previously. The celebrants eventually retired. The next day, Commander MacMillan felt moved to apologize to those ashore for the *Peary*'s rather serious breach of the peace.

An impromptu race using dories with outboard motors was held on July fourth between members of the *Bowdoin* and *Peary* crews. The remainder of the holiday was spent relaxing and recovering from the farewell party. Herrmann and Grosvenor left for the south on schedule and one last party was held aboard the *Peary* for the nurses.

Although the coastal ice pack was still in place, MacMillan decided to move both ships north to the most southerly Inuit Eskimo village of Hopedale, knowing that the ships would have to "buck ice" most of the way. The nurses left the *Peary* at midnight, 4–5 July, and the ships stood out to sea at 1:30 A.M. The very early dawn of 5 July reminded everyone that the expedition was approaching the "Land of the Midnight Sun." The *Bowdoin* led the *Peary* until dark, then fell astern and took position off the *Peary*'s port quarter. Lieutenant Schur noted that icebergs, a remarkable sight only a week before, were now both routine and too numerous to count; he also wrote that "they still look great when the moon's rays strike them." At 10:30 P.M. dense fog enveloped the two vessels and they immediately hove to, unable to dodge icebergs in this preradar era.

During the short period of darkness the fog lifted, and at dawn the watch reported the beginnings of the Arctic ice pack ahead. Again, Lieutenant Schur provided by far the best description:

July 6th, 1924. At Sea Enroute Hopedale, Lab.
Underway at . . . steaming on various courses, *Bowdoin* again taking the lead at daylight—several seal and whale were seen by the 1st Mate Freeman.

The morning was spent in taking pictures both movies and still and admiring the beautiful floe of drift ice which at first seems as tho it would be impossible to penetrate, also in a distant [sic] large bergs were seen.

It is most interesting to note in the distant [sic] what seems like enormous icebergs, changing shape and colors, but upon getting nearer they turned out to be only mirages.

At 11:30 A.M. communication was established by voice with *Bowdoin*, first time since leaving that two way radio communication has been established, McDonald is delighted and is certainly talking about it. Our Capt. Steele, an old Glouschester fishing capt. was called into the radio room to receive directions from MacMillan on the *Bowdoin* re directions for getting through the solid mass of drift ice, when told to speak to MacMillan he promptly said

"Hello Captain" into the mouth piece and was surprised that MacMillan did not carry the conversation as per city telephone.

The afternoon is upon us, here we are forced to hit the solid mass of ice at a reduced speed, the ship certainly does tremble and we rejoice that all ports have been covered over with steel, off in the distant [*sic*] Labrador can be plainly seen, the ice pack extending to sea as far as the eye can see, it is a great sight, not so cold, the air is dry and temp. +45 [degrees Fahrenheit]. As yet, we have not reached the great open spaces where icebergs are bergs.

As the ship continues on its way northward fighting its way through the dense ice drift, the air is much warmer, at times it reaches a temperature of +60, this is caused by the land breeze coming over the bleak rocky land called Labrador . . .

About 3:30 P.M. the *Bowdoin* ran on top of a large floe of ice and was forced to sally ship and go full speed astern, apparently no damage done . . .

. . . 8:00 P.M. . . . We are now losing most of the ice and are running close ashore, the west wind seems to be forcing the ice to sea.

Near Disaster Near Hopedale

At 10:30 P.M. on 6 July, both ships anchored in the lee of Cape Strawberry and MacMillan ordered rest for all hands and equipment. They were to get under way at 6:00 A.M. The next day, 7 July, was to prove pivotal to the entire expedition, especially for those aboard the heavily overloaded *Peary*. Text from an undated *Boston Globe* clipping in the Schur papers set the stage for what was to happen:

The *Peary* left Boston with an unusually heavy load and at Wiscasset this burden was increased until the ship, built as a minesweeper, was exceedingly low in the water. On her hurricane deck, aft, she carried the three amphibian planes in special cradles, while spare wings in their huge crates, spare engines and spare propellers were piled everywhere. With the exception of a narrow alleyway all of the main deck aft of the companionway was piled with drums of gasoline and the forward deck bore four spare boats.

At Sydney, however, this load was greatly increased. The coalbunkers were filled to capacity, piles of fuel were placed here and there about the decks and many additional tons in bags were laid atop the gasoline drums.

On 7 July 1925, the expedition suffered near disaster as the unusually heavy-laden *Peary* ran hard aground on previously uncharted rocks off the Labrador coast, near Hopedale. Note the list to starboard.
Schur Family Papers

So deep was the *Peary* in the water that the start from Sydney was delayed until workman could rivet and weld heavy steel plates over the lower port-holes. This proved to be a wise precaution, in view of the heavy weather encountered, as these portholes were under water practically all the trip.

At all events the *Peary* left Sydney more deeply laden than her builders ever intended she should be: in fact, after she returned to Labrador veteran fishermen who had watched her sail from there stated that they never believed she would return.

Lieutenant Schur's account of the day provides details of the near disaster:

July 7, 1924. Anchored Off Dunn's Is., Labrador.
1:00 P.M. finds me on the forecastle pointing out rocks to Reber for pastime, we are following *Bowdoin*. *Peary*'s position off *Bowdoin* Port Quarter distance 200 yards, everything looks well, our speed in about 4 knots, Captain George Steele at wheel, McDonald on bridge with Steele, sky clear, wind NW velocity 48 MPH quite a sea running, promptly at 1:40 the *Peary* struck a[n

uncharted] rocky shoal, running high and dry, the ship listing 40 degrees to port, the jar certainly did upset everything on the ship, people running around deck as though mad, the radio operator McGee rushed into the radio room and called *Bowdoin* telling them to come near us as we were on the rocks, the wind and sea lifting the stern up and down, and it certainly did look bad, tears were in the eyes of the Navy men on board, because after the hard work done to prepare for this trip, it now looked like our trip to the Arctic would end here on the rocky shoals off eastern end of Kayaksaulik Island. Captain George Steele here demonstrated his superior ability to handle a situation which certainly was bad; his cool, calm and quick estimate of the situation, and his seaman like handling of his rudder and engines and lines certainly were alone responsible for the refloating of the *Peary*.

The *Bowdoin* immediately swinging around and running alongside the *Peary*, Steele having had a line secured to the crosstrees of the fore mast lead to the *Bowdoin*'s stern, likewise a stern line, the *Bowdoin* heaving on line forcing the *Peary* from her 40 degree list to Port to a 50 degree list to Starboard.

Captain Steele with the aid of the Navy officers and men lowered the Starboard life boat under great difficulties, taking on board a kedge anchor from our Starboard bow and running it well out and placing it broad off the Starboard bow, the water depth forward was one fathom on Port bow and 6 fathoms on Starboard bow.

The ship's crew certainly is excited, some have already packed their belongings, others have had only one thought that being to secure around themselves a good life preserver. Our Doctor was rather amusing appearing from below with a life belt on and carrying his suitcase, likewise Mr. Koelz came on deck with a back pack and 22 rifle, with a life belt securely adjusted for his body.

In the life boat with Capt. Steele is our ship's cook, a very able cook likewise a good seaman, upon leaving the ship's side to place the kedge anchor, he cried out to one of the men on deck, "Watch the bread in the oven don't let it burn."

At 2:15 the second attempt is made to refloat the *Peary*. Heaving in on the forward kedge line and the *Bowdoin* hauling on stern line, tide rising we were able to float the *Peary*, but only after desperate tugging and hauling on all lines and backing full speed with our engine and promptly at 3:00 P.M. we slid back off rocks.

During our tense and unhappy moments spent on the rocks, one had only to glance around and note the landlubbers, and unseaman like qualities of people on board.

Barometer 29.32 wind NW velocity 49 MPH rough sea ships head 329 degrees. The life boat which was used in placing our kedge anchors was secured astern and when backing down was smashed under the stern, McDonald getting a good dunking during this operation. The life boat capsizing, all oars and equipment being lost in the sea, the *Bowdoin* picking the life boat up and secured it on her deck.

Hopedale

In his report from Hopedale to the National Geographic Society, Commander McDonald noted that the ice had cleared just four days previously and that the Canadian government mailboat was still frozen solid in its winter harbor some miles to the south. The MacMillan expedition ships were the first to call at Hopedale since October 1924.

Byrd's journal for 8 July revealed another near-disaster for the expedition:

Had a very serious escape from death a few minutes ago. Gray and McGee had just run a heavy copper wire uninsulated cable from the radio room across the gangway about the height of my head. They were trying it out with 100,000 volts and watching and listening to . . . any one passing by. I had on rubber shoes and was coming from aft behind their radio room door which was half open so that they neither heard nor saw me. My head got six inches from that wire before I was stopped and the 100,000 volts would have jumped to my head had I gotten one inch nearer! Gray was white as a sheet. There another narrow squeak. The gods of . . . [sic] have been good to me. That wire will have to be well insulated.

The expedition stayed at Hopedale for two-and-a-half days. The primary purpose of the stop was to obtain tailored, fully furred Arctic wear for the flight crews from the local Inuit women. This Arctic wear, especially the sealskin boots of the Labrador Inuit, was considered superior to that made by their kinsmen in Greenland. By the end of the brief stay, not just the flight crews, but almost every man aboard had a set of these glamorous and very practical clothes made by the Inuit seamstresses. Commander McDonald even commissioned a child's set for his nephew, Eugene Kinney.

All of the surviving journals record the party's shock at the extreme poverty of the Inuit of the Labrador coast, and remark on the critical and selfless role played by the few Moravian missionaries present. At Hopedale, the southernmost Inuit settlement, there were 160 Inuit and eight Moravian missionaries, counting the missionaries' families. McDonald was particularly affected by the situation and immediately cabled his sister Florence in Chicago with instructions to purchase "toys for 76 Eskimo kiddies, half boys, half girls. These toys are to serve as Christmas presents for the Eskimo kiddies all along the Labrador under the Moravians who are doing wonderful work." He also instructed her to purchase a Santa suit. McDonald urged Florence to send everything quickly so that the gifts made the mail boats before the season closed. He also wired his friend Fred Corley, merchandising manager for Marshall Field, telling him:

> I saw myriads of toy Eskimo dolls made by the Eskimos in their crude fashion animals including seal caribou wolf polar bear canoes dog whips and dogs carved out of wood some of them excellently done by Eskimo children of ten years of age ... the kiddies have been taught that there is a Santa Claus and they know him as Father Christmas ... Would you not like to put in a section of a window showing some of these toys made by the Labrador Eskimos and then be instrumental in arranging an exchange of gifts between the Chicago school children and the Eskimo children of Labrador.

Typical of Gene McDonald, this largesse was kept completely private.

While at Hopedale, McDonald, obviously excited by the success of the radio operations to that point, reported to Zenith:

> Radio working great on short waves we are sure making history we receive our daily newspaper not only from the states but from Nauen Germany we can send a message to the states anytime of day or night we are using phone [rather than Morse code] exclusively between the *Bowdoin* and the *Peary* we have constant communications and can reach each other anytime at will without prearranged schedule this is the first time this has been done by radio between two ships for instance the *Bowdoin* may be miles and miles

away from us yet I have only to go to the radio room pick up the transmitter which is built like a telephone set it on the prearranged wave length which we use exclusively for intercommunications start the generators going and say with voice into the transmitter this is wap calling wnp Reinartz hears me calling over a loud speaker connected in their forecastle and comes to his transmitter I then ask for commander MacMillan tell him the speed were making ask him what port he would like to have us make that night and get my answer immediately by voice . . .

Although eminently successful for intership communications, a potential radio or radio operator problem surfaced on 8 July while the ships were in Hopedale when the following cable was sent by a vice president of the National Geographic Society to MacMillan:

> Please have Reinartz respond Navy Station NKF on schedule time stop Navy Bellevue station hears him but cannot reach him stop important personal message for you stop Geographic without news of expedition two days as though personal communications from expedition sent and heard regularly stop please try to get thru brief message to Geographic every night and every morning early if possible stop unable here to give information about location of vessels and progress stop please have WNP instruct amateur receiving each message to wire us collect stop

MacMillan explained the lack of contact in this case as due to repair work being performed on the radios. However, the sporadic quality of official radio communication, apparently caused by some expedition radio operators having heightened interest in amateur messages, continued to plague the expedition until the problem was solved several weeks later.[1]

The expedition entertained many Inuit visitors aboard both vessels at Hopedale who had come to trade for souvenirs and local crafts. The Inuit were fascinated when they were able to talk to their kinfolk on the other ship via radio and were convinced that there were wires running between them.

Radio took a more serious role when McDonald learned that the old-fashioned battery-operated receiver at the Hopedale mission had run out of batteries in the fall of 1924. The most recent news of the world had come to this isolated mission via dogsled almost three months previously. McDonald had the expedition radio operators upgrade the circuitry of the old mission radio and change out obsolete tubes and batteries for state-of-the-art units. He reported that the old receiver and batteries would provide only twenty-four hours of total service, but that the new set-up would provide at least three hundred hours of continuous service on one set of batteries. McDonald left multiple sets of batteries and tubes behind. Other records indicate that McDonald provided battery-powered sets for the isolated Moravian missions for years to come.[2]

On the afternoon of 10 July, with fur clothing and memorabilia aboard, the expedition sailed north to Windy Tickle (on the Labrador coast, sailor's jargon identifies "tickles" as narrow passages where unpredictable winds and strong currents make sailing hazardous or "ticklish") at the mouth of Jack Lane's Bay. The purpose of this final stop on Labrador's rugged shore was to pick up Abram Bromfield, who had accompanied MacMillan on the 1923–24 expedition and was an expert interpreter of the Inuhuit language. Upon arrival at Windy Tickle, MacMillan and McDonald took one of the motor dories and traveled eighteen miles up the bay to the Bromfield homestead. Both Abram and his seventy-year-old father had been born on the Labrador coast and had spent their entire lives there. The next morning the party returned, followed closely by the entire Bromfield clan in their larger boat. The day turned into a picnic, with the Bromfields providing venison steaks, trout, and entertainment; in return, the expedition's doctor held an informal clinic for the family.

Commander McDonald's 12 July report to the National Geographic Society best tells the story of that evening:

Between the hours of ten and eleven last evening there was broadcast a radio vocal and instrumental program the entire concert being supplied by the venerable Samuel Bromfield, the Game Warden, Governor, Mayor, Chief of Police, Fire Marshall, Post Master and also one seventh of the population of Jack Lane's Bay in other words the population of Jack Lane's Bay totals seven Period Sam hearing we were in port came down with his high hat and fiddle and played jig after jig in which his heels knees and legs were as essential a part to the music as his fiddle he sang and he posed for his photograph Period Commander MacMillan gave a short address over the radio period Mr. Bromfield's son Abram again accompanies us as Eskimo interpreter he having been north on previous trips with MacMillan. Communication between the *Bowdoin* and the *Peary* is now by schedule maintained on forty and eighty meters at the hours of eight [in the] morning, one and seven [in the] afternoon.

Commander Byrd became troubled by the apparent lack of urgency on MacMillan's part to get the expedition to Etah. The exchange of messages during this time led to an agreement between Byrd, MacMillan, and McDonald to "reduce to writing all material communications." (The level of historical detail of this expedition that has survived is due, in large part, to this decision.) After a request by Byrd to make better progress, MacMillan responded in an uncharacteristically strong fashion:

> I note your request that every effort be made to reach the edge of the ice pack as soon as possible to take advantage of the possibility of getting through the ice should it open. I fully realize the importance of so doing and have realized it on every one of my Arctic trips. Since the Expedition is to return in the fall this is absolutely necessary to give us sufficient time to accomplish the objects of our expedition.
>
> For your information let me state that in all the history of Arctic work I know of but one expedition to ever reach Etah before August first. To attempt to do this much before this date will result in a tremendous waste of fuel and possibly failure of the mission. The *Peary* has a three thousand two hundred mile cruising radius and no more; this must be conserved to the fullest extent. The only rational way to do this is to await open water in Melville Bay. My plans are based upon Peary's experience of 18 years. On his last and successful trip with eighty two degrees thirty minutes as his objective he left New York City July sixth and Sydney N.S. July sixteenth. We are now at least twelve days ahead of time and following our departure from Disco it is reasonable to assume we shall have a clean run through the Bay to Cape York without undue consumption of coal. If we had an unlimited supply we should now be at the edge of the pack awaiting an opportunity to get through the leads. Your anxiety to reach Etah is but natural and is shared by us all.

We are leaving at one o'clock for Cape Mugford, one hundred and thirty miles north from which point we take our departure for the Greenland Coast, there to load on as much coal as possible and as quickly as possible and proceed northward.

Byrd's journal entry for 12 July told of yet another near disaster to the expedition:

While standing on the bridge about 2 P.M. taking some sights I saw some thick smoke coming from amidships. I was there in a jiffy and found a pile of life preservers on fire. They were piled against one of the wooden wing crates near plane NA-1. I threw one of the preservers overboard and put the fire extinguisher on the rest of them. As I wrote the day we hit the rock we are already short on life preservers so the incident is unfortunate, but, it could have been so much worse. Another minute and the flame would have ignited the oil and kerosene. The place is soaked in and nothing in the world could have saved this ship from 7600 gallons of gasoline around her decks. As a result of this fire McDonald has agreed with my recommendation to put on a fire watch including the personnel of the naval unit and the doctors Gayer and Kelty.

Dangerous Crossing: Davis Strait

At two o'clock on the morning of 13 July, all hands were rousted and both ships weighed anchor. MacMillan immediately discovered that the *Bowdoin*'s mechanically complex featherable propeller was broken.[3] Although the *Bowdoin* was a sailing ship, she relied on her powerful engine to drive her through the ice floes. After confirming that the prop was damaged and must be replaced, MacMillan established a radio schedule between the *Peary* and the *Bowdoin* (8:00 A.M., 1:00 P.M., and 7:00 P.M. on forty meters) and sent the *Peary* ahead. MacMillan planned to beach the *Bowdoin* and change the prop at Windy Tickle. Unfortunately, the beach at Windy Tickle proved to be far too rocky and the *Bowdoin*'s crew spent a very long day being towed all the way back to Hopedale by the Bromfield launch.

Meanwhile, the *Peary* had spent an equally long day ramming her way through the soft but still very dangerous ice pack, tying up to the ice pack itself off Cape Mugford for the few hours of darkness. Further radio messages were passed back and forth over the two hundred plus miles separating the ships, and the *Peary* was ordered to proceed northeast across the six-hundred-mile Davis Strait to Disko Island and Godhavn, Greenland.[4] The *Bowdoin* party expected to replace the prop and follow in about twenty-four hours. Ultimately, the *Bowdoin*'s crew had to wait in Hopedale for over a week for the arrival of lower tides to expose the propeller. The *Peary* complement, particularly the navy fliers, was quite concerned about the *Bowdoin*'s difficulties since there was no possibility of accomplishing the goals of the expedition without MacMillan's expertise and without the vital aviation gasoline stored on the deck of the *Bowdoin*.

At dawn, 1:30 A.M. on 13 July,[5] the *Peary* turned her bow northeast and began to ram her way through solid pack ice. As she proceeded through the pack, Schur noted "the early sun shines upon the ice, radiating some of the most delicate iridescent colors forth." After two hours of steady progress, the *Peary* broke free of the pack ice into open water and increased speed.

The crossing was uneventful, with calm seas and beautiful weather. Schur described the sunset on 14 July: "Tonight was the prettiest sunset that I have ever seen, sun setting at 10:15, rising again at 11:30. I was able to sit on deck and read without aid of any lights tonight, it never did get dark." By the time the sun was fully up, the hills of southern Greenland were visible on the eastern horizon. The *Peary* made her way north up the coast all day, surrounded by hundreds of icebergs. Before he gave up, Schur counted eighty-two bergs, some over three hundred feet high.

The following morning at 5:30 A.M. they picked up the local marine pilots for Godhavn harbor. The crew had been looking forward to some "real liberty," having heard of the friendly nature of the Danish officials, their families, and the Inuhuit residents. The town dances of Godhavn ("good harbor") were known to all northern sailors. McDonald and Captain Steele were anxious to replenish the *Peary*'s almost depleted coal supply and to make ready for the run north to Etah, the most dangerous part of the voyage.

Godhavn, Fuel, and Conspiracy

The pilots guided the *Peary* into a section of Godhavn harbor known as Englishmen's Bay and they dropped anchor at midmorning, 16 July 1925. Schur described a rather desolate scene, the mountains and shore made mostly of rock, with very little vegetation and lots of snow. Schur noted that the homes of the Danish officials were built of wood, painted red with white trim and gray roofs, while nearby Inuhuit homes were constructed of sod and wood.

Soon after the *Peary* arrived, the governor of Godhavn, Mr. Malmquist, the governor of North Greenland, Mr. Rosendahl, and the local doctor came aboard. They were all Danes; only the physician spoke a little English. With a great deal of difficulty, McDonald was able to make clear that the *Peary* was part of the MacMillan expedition. That hurdle cleared, the governor of North Greenland expressed surprise that the expedition was headed north to Etah. He had been told only that MacMillan was coming to inspect old Norse ruins in southern Greenland, and no mention had been made of the *Peary* at all. This was doubly serious for the expedition because, though the *Bowdoin* burned oil and was self-sufficient, the *Peary* had to acquire additional coal either to be able to return home or to continue north. An extended discussion revealed that there was quarantine on the village due to whooping cough. Because no one could go ashore, the *Peary* would not be able to obtain coal. Although the discussion was friendly—in fact, the two officials had breakfast aboard—there was to be no liberty and no coal. The governors explained that a ship had called recently and had taken aboard most of the available coal. As a result, there was not enough coal in Godhavn for the coming winter. The situation appeared desperate. If a solution to the coal problem could not be found, one of the two major goals of the expedition—air exploration of the Polar Sea—could not occur, since the *Peary*, which carried the planes, could proceed no further north.

Commander McDonald began at once to solve the problem by making maximum use of both diplomacy and shortwave radio. On the diplomatic front, he maintained cordial relations with the Danes, meeting with them daily and drafting an almost continuous stream of notes and letters to Governor Rosendahl. McDonald expressed understanding and sympathy for the problems the coal shortage caused the local community. He proposed moving the *Peary* some sixty miles to the coal mines at Umanak and suggested using the entire crew to mine the eighty tons necessary for the *Peary.* He even assured the governor that they would be glad to pay full price for the coal that they themselves would mine.

McDonald was determined to leave no stone unturned. Thanks exclusively to the fact that shortwave radio alone could span long distances even in full daylight, he was able to communicate with MacMillan back in Hopedale, with the National Geographic Society and the U.S. Navy in Washington, and with numerous contacts in Chicago.

Although McDonald and, to a lesser degree, Lieutenant Commander Byrd, were quite busy trying to extricate the expedition, the rest of the men were at loose ends. For the first time on the voyage, Lieutenant Schur's journal shows the stress the men were under. His usually voluble and extensive daily entries soon were reduced to a few terse lines per day to record the passage of time:

July 16
. . . There certainly are a downhearted bunch on board tonight. After enduring a trip upon the rocks, seasickness and hard work so far, here in little Greenland a man of foreign birth informs us that he can not give us any coal unless the crown of Denmark says so. So here we are, anchored in Disko Bay, two months food supply, 70 tons of coal, no liberty and a few hundred tons of the much needed coal at Umanak a few miles north of here. The radio sure will be hot for the next few days to Washington. There being no darkness it is hard to sleep now, it is not unusual to find us up around one A.M. in the morning.

July 17
. . . We are all still hot over the coal and liberty question, it seems that the Quarantine works only one way, we are not allowed to go ashore, still the Eskimos are allowed to come to the ship to trade, also the Danish men come on board to visit, some good old American names have been used by the crew to describe how mean a trick they are playing on us.

McDonald is now keeping up a conversation by letter with the Governor, only today he sent a boat ashore with Gray and Francis on board with the American flag astern and the Naval Reserve flag flying in the bow just to put on a little dog.

July 18. Still at Disko Is.
Just awaiting developments.
No coal,
No liberty,
No pictures,
No MacMillan.
Bowdoin still at Hopedale, Labrador changing propellers. MacMillan said he would leave Hopedale at 1:00 A.M. Sunday.

July 19
Weather cloudy, raining mountain tops covered with new snow. Everyone on board rather quiet, we were in hopes of being able to go ashore today and see the Eskimo women in their beaded dress, from the ship a few are seen walking around. Byrd, McDonald and the governor of North Greenland are sending each other notes, we are trying every known means to procure coal to continue our voyage. Reber and I went walking over the hills this P.M. after which we rowed a few miles.

July 20. Anchored at Godhavn, Greenland.
Uneventful.
Crew exercised by hiking and rowing.
Anchored at Godhavn, Greenland.
We are still marking time, waiting for word to reach the governor of North Greenland to supply us with coal—we are all aware that the National Geographic will have word here in a few days.

The irrepressible McDonald seems to be one of the few whose morale was unaffected by the *Peary's* predicament. He used the time to answer correspondence from the United States via shortwave radio, to purchase an authentic skin kayak from a local artisan, and to become proficient at maneuvering the fragile and unstable craft. In a radiogram to H. H. Roemer of Zenith, McDonald remarked, "Am now an expert with a kayak beat a native Eskimo and two men pulling a rowboat today."

It is obvious from his correspondence, however, that McDonald was very concerned. He wired Sport Herrmann, newly returned to Chicago after leaving the expedition at Battle Harbor, and asked him to help the National Geographic Society organize a relief ship carrying 125 tons of coal and fifteen barrels of kerosene or fuel oil. Had the relief ship been necessary, the *Peary* would have had to go north to Etah without a tenth of enough food for the winter (if they got frozen in) and no coal at all to get back south to meet a collier there.

The crew had another object lesson to contemplate as they swung at anchor in Godhavn harbor: the battered and twisted old hulk that had been the Arctic rescue ship, the *Fox*. Sir Leopold McClintock had set out on her in 1857 to discover the fate of the twenty-eight-man Franklin party that had disappeared into the Northwest Passage in 1845. In 1857, the *Fox* had sailed from England, pausing at Godhavn, just like the *Peary*, before setting out through the perilous ice of Melville Bay. They made their way through the bay until, on 13 August, the pack came in solid around them and they were locked fast. For six months, they remained frozen in the ice as they drifted over one thousand miles southward. When the *Fox* broke free in the spring, she limped into Godhavn for repairs and eventually did discover the fate of the Franklin party. In later years, she was sold to the Danish government and used in these waters until she was, once again, almost crushed by the ice in Melville Bay. This time she was towed to Godhavn, beached, and left to rot. If the MacMillan expedition ever did get coal, it had to sail dead center across four hundred miles of that same Melville Bay, through the same ice pack at the same time of year as the *Fox*. Every man knew that, and every man also knew that the expedition could only carry provisions for three months because of the space and weight taken up by the Loening Amphibians and their mass of spare parts.

Byrd, frustrated by the delay of the whole trip to this point, and especially the delay at Godhavn, sent another strongly worded message to MacMillan on 22 July that showed not only his frustration but also his lack of knowledge of polar conditions:

Feel it my duty to call your attention to extreme seriousness of situation from an aviation standpoint that has arisen from the valuable time now being lost. I tell you most solemnly that unless we leave immediately for Etah all the aviation personnel consider that the superhuman effort they are ready to put into their jobs will probably avail nothing. I most urgently recommend that if necessary heroic measures be resorted to get the *Peary* on its way to Etah even though coal must reach us after we get there. I warn you that all the labor effort and money put into this expedition will probably be wasted unless the *Peary* leaves right away for Etah. Can you not tow the *Peary* part of the way back here if she has not enough coal to get up to Etah and back? There is [*sic*] over twenty-six thousand pounds of gasoline oil food and other equipment that must be taken by aircraft to the first base in order to get the necessary quantity of gasoline to the base and the Polar Sea. You understand also that it will take over a week to set the three planes up and get them ready for the first flight to the first base. Each plane can drop only a little over 500 pounds each trip to the second base. I realize that you and McDonald have done everything humanly possible to get the Danish Government to give the Governor here instructions to supply coal he has refused. But it now seems to me that we should wait no longer. There is no telling how long it will take to get a decision and get it to the Governor here. His radio station is not finished, and he seems to experience some difficulty in getting messages.

McDonald could not have put more effort into getting word to Washington. At some point on the seventh day spent anchored in Godhavn Harbor, it became clear to McDonald that Governor Rosendahl could supply coal, or at least grant permission to mine it at Umanak, if only the Danish government gave its permission—and that could be gotten via their embassy in Washington. It was not possible, of course, to contact the embassy with the local Danish longwave transmitter until nightfall, and nightfall was several months hence! There are several versions of what happened next.

One version, which appeared in newspapers in several places, is that Rosendahl and McDonald contacted the Danish embassy in Washington using the *Peary*'s shortwave equipment. A young radio amateur in Washington received the message and relayed it to the embassy. In another version, Byrd and McDonald used the shortwave equipment to contact the navy in Washington. The navy (and perhaps the State Department) then contacted the Danish embassy asking for permission for the Greenlandic authorities to sell coal to the *Peary.* In each story, the permission was granted and the message returned to Godhavn in about four hours.

The document that approaches primary historical evidence is a daily report sent by McDonald to the National Geographic Society on 24 July:

> Many thanks for your wonderful cooperation in expediting official message to and from Danish Minister. Governor Rosendahl sent message from *Peary* to Washington via 9XN [the powerful Zenith factory station in Chicago] at two A.M. Friday received response a few moments ago ten-thirty same night. It made the governor feel most happy he is on board the *Peary* in my state-room as I dictate this, and we are enroute Umanak for coal having left Disko Godhavn nine A.M. and should arrive Umanak mines at seven A.M. tomorrow Saturday. Mines are surface mines within twenty feet of shore; we should be loaded in twenty-four hours even with crude loading facilities. Governor Rosendahl deserves great credit for cooperation he has extended us on very ambiguous advice. He, however, immediately upon receipt of the official communication from Secretary of Navy to Commander Byrd advising Danish cooperation thru American Minister, agreed to give us the coal and to expedite delivery came with us we are towing his little auxiliary schooner so that he may return from Umanak. He brought with him aboard also famous Eskimo Pilot Peter Dalager and Aage Bretting, Danish Engineering Consular for the Government of Greenland. Norwegian steamship *Danelac* arrived Godhavn just before our sailing, but Governor Rosendahl realizing time emergency came with *Peary* regardless. Immediately after loading we will head north and join *Bowdoin* that left Godhavn at eleven A.M. someplace north—they traveling under sail only and not going into Umanak with us.

It is quite possible that all versions of this incident are based on fact. Certainly after McDonald understood that all which stood between the *Peary* and coal was permission from the Danish government's representatives in Washington (rather than in Copenhagen, which had no shortwave radio), he and Byrd would have been making the *Peary*'s radio "hot," as Lieutenant Schur said, sending a flood of messages to Washington. Worrying about which version of this story is the most accurate simply clouds the main issue; this incident, by itself, demonstrated the vast superiority of shipboard communication *using the shortwave spectrum* over both the longwave and medium wave spectrums, then in standard use. If the expedition had proceeded no farther north, the practical use of shortwave, demonstrated in this real-life emergency, would have proved the expedition a success and doubtless would have affected the future development of navy fleet communications.

The last entries in Lieutenant Schur's journal recorded the trip to the Umanak coal mine:

July 24, 1925. Godhavn, Greenland.
MacMillan and McDonald went into conference, and it was decided to shove off as soon as the Governor arrived on board; well he arrived bag and baggage at 7:30 our time, in the meantime his launch was secured astern, we are to tow it to the mines, he will return on board it to Godhavn.

Underway at . . . we sure are balling the jack to the mines, during the day routine work is being carried out on board, the Governor and his aides, his interpreter and his Eskimo pilot, go at great length to explain the weather, coast and are playing up to us in order to stand in straight, he claims he did not know that the Navy was to assist MacMillan. But I feel as though he has delayed our progress quite some. In the evenings our radio class in session [the flight crews were practicing Morse code for use while in the air, or should they be forced down].

July 25, 1925. At Sea Enroute to Coal Mine near Umanak, Greenland.
Reber and I up early and enjoying the rock hills of Greenland where they get the Green is more than I know, there is very little of it to be seen, mostly rocks and snow and sea, I really don't think that one of America's Real Estate Sharks could dispose of this place. As we steam between the various islands a seal here and there pops its head up for air, then submerges again, at 6:00 A.M. the mine is in sight, there seems to be at least 800 tons of coal piled up on the beach.

As soon as the coal was loaded at Umanak, cordial farewells were said, and the *Peary* put on steam to catch up with the *Bowdoin,* already well up the coast, heading for the village of South Upernavik. MacMillan had taken the *Bowdoin* north soon after the *Peary* left Godhavn, believing that the more powerful engines of the *Peary* would enable her to catch up. MacMillan, McDonald, and Byrd were anxious to reach Etah by 1 August. MacMillan knew that the three-week-long "summer season" at Etah and nearby Smith Sound almost always began on the first of August; they needed every minute of those three weeks if all of the goals of the expedition were to be achieved before the ice closed back in for the year.

The Melville Bay Ice Pack

The chance of danger was particularly high in the waters directly west of Greenland, Baffin Bay, and Melville Bay. Erik Erngaard, in *Greenland: Then and Now*, wrote that Melville Bay had long been known to sailors as Greenland's Graveyard and noted that the 1819 whaling fleet lost fourteen ships to the dreaded Melville Bay ice pack. In 1821 eleven ships and in 1822 seven ships were crushed in the ice pack. The record year, however, was 1830 when an enormous iceberg embedded in the pack suddenly overturned (as often happens); in less than fifteen minutes the entire Melville Bay whaling fleet of nineteen ships was reduced to "matchwood." There were also several instances of individual ships (most notably the British rescue vessel, *Fox*) becoming imprisoned in the Melville Bay ice pack for more than a year before being released. MacMillan's description, in the November 1925 *National Geographic*, of the expedition's passage across the Melville Bay ice pack reads like a Jack London novel:

> As both ships proceeded northward, we encountered our first ice off South Upernivik, a scattered field, through which we easily passed. A half hour later we met the real pack—hard blue ice five feet thick. We were glad to follow the *Peary* slowly smashing through it with her reinforced steel-concrete bow. Finally conditions were such that we tied up to a large sheet to await better luck . . . With a change of tide, the leads began to open up.
>
> We fought the pack all day, the *Bowdoin* generally following the more powerful *Peary*, which split big pans wide open. When dealing with the solid, unbroken pack ice, the *Bowdoin* was far inferior to her big sister, but in loosely packed ice, in narrow leads with sharp turns, the *Bowdoin* left the *Peary* almost hull down. At 6 o'clock we were free of the ice and stopped our

In late July, both ships were temporarily trapped in the dreaded Melville Bay ice pack. Here, the *Peary* is immobilized by what appear to be relatively thin but continuous ice floes.
Schur Family Papers

engines for 45 minutes to await the *Peary*. At 11:30 we were again in the midst of it, slowly working westward toward Cape York.

On July 29 little progress was made. We did not know which way to turn, since a thick fog prevented intelligent ice pilotage . . .

The 30th [of July 1925] was a hard day for both ships. The *Bowdoin* was so tightly wedged that the *Peary* was called upon to extricate her from the jaws of huge ice pans. As it happened, I spent the day conning the *Peary* through the ice, and therefore had a good opportunity to witness the *Bowdoin* in action—a wonderful sight. Like a thing alive, she twisted and turned through the leads, and when meeting a floe which she could not avoid, fairly leaped out of the water, her clean-cut bow shooting up to such an angle that it seemed as if she were coming out bodily on top of the ice.

Finally the *Peary*, strong as she is, was absolutely helpless. Four times she had hurled herself at full speed into a crack between two tremendous pans,

The *Bowdoin* is seen moored to the Melville Bay ice, awaiting an open lead in near whiteout conditions.
Schur Family Papers

Tung-we and Ma-mo-na greet the *Peary* near the Crimson Cliffs on the
approaches to Etah. The vertical object on the horizon is the *Bowdoin* coming
up to join the faster *Peary*.

Schur Family Papers

hoping so to shatter the edges that she might squeeze through. The *Bowdoin* circled about in a narrow basin, jockeying for a dash at the rift made by the bigger ship the instant the latter cleared the narrow opening. The last time, the *Peary* became so tightly wedged that her 9-foot, 4-bladed propeller failed to back her out. We stopped engines, put out ice anchors, and awaited a change of wind and tide. Our best was not enough.

The Arctic is full of surprises, the largest of which is the sudden change in ice conditions . . . At 10 the *Peary* started through the lead without the help of the engine! So rapidly was she moving that we ran a towline to the *Bowdoin*, snuggling under the red, white, and blue tails of the planes, as if afraid of being left behind. At five the next morning we were again under way, breaking out through the pack into open water and heading straight to Cape York, the hard-fought goal at the end of the Melville Bay ice field.

Cape York was blocked with ice and clearly inaccessible . . . Shortly after passing Conical Rock we encountered a fog so dense that we narrowly missed several large bergs looming mountain like in the mist. The *Peary*, being longer, does not respond as quickly to her helm as the *Bowdoin*. She was therefore in greater danger of collision . . . A radio request from Captain Steele that we lay to for a while was readily complied with, since the compasses on both ships were extremely sluggish and at times varied by 20 to 30 degrees.

The fog soon lifted, and we hastened on to Etah, where we arrived in a snowstorm, three hours ahead of schedule, on August 1. My plans were for the arrival on this date and for the departure about August 25, but not later than September 1. Since the crews of our ships numbered 39 men and we were only provisioned for three months, an enforced wintering in the North, by one or both, would be a serious matter.

FOUR

Etah at Last

*M*acMILLAN EXPECTED TO FIND THE USUAL twenty to thirty members of the Inuhuit community in residence at Etah, but when the expedition arrived, the seminomadic band was scattered in coastal hunting camps throughout the region. Within two hours, however, two old friends of MacMillan's, Noo-ka-ping-wa and In-you-gee-to, arrived by kayak, and the important contact with the local Inuhuit residents was made.

Byrd and the aviators had expected to find a fairly large beach at Etah, even at high tide. They had planned to use this beach both to assemble the Loenings and as a normal seaplane parking ramp. This was not to be. A quick survey revealed that the only stretch of the shore that could even be called a "beach" was very small, very steep, and strewn with large rocks and boulders. The beach was entirely unsuitable for a parking ramp since it almost disappeared at high tide. After what must have been a very intense discussion, it became clear that the beach, no matter how unsuitable, was the only place where the Loenings could be assembled. The beach would have to be cleared of the larger rocks and boulders and a ramp would have to be constructed. If the ramp were smooth enough, the entire party, pulling together, might be able to haul each fuselage up to the top of the beach for assembly.

The wings of the Loenings had come north on the *Peary* in large plywood crates. None of the surviving records indicate which member of the expedition suggested using the sides of these crates as a ramp surface, but that suggestion proved to be the difference between success and failure for the Naval Arctic Unit.

After a short "night" of rest, all hands began the arduous task of unloading and assembling the three Loening Amphibians early on the morning of

Assembling the three Loening Amphibians at Etah was a difficult task performed under most trying circumstances. A raft was constructed using two of the *Peary* lifeboats and the side panel of one of the large wing crates. The wings and their crates were then floated ashore, and a ramp for the aircraft was constructed using the dismantled wing crates (2 August 1925).
Schur Family and U.S. Navy

The fuselage of NA-2 was hauled up the steep ramp by all hands, 2 August 1925. Schur and Byrd are second and third in the line, In-you-gee-to is fifth in line, and McDonald is ninth, facing the camera.

Schur Family and U.S. Navy

Looking east up Foulke Fjord, 2 August 1925. The partially assembled NA-2 is in the foreground. The *Peary* with the other two fuselages is visible in the background.

Schur Family and U.S. Navy

NA-2 is assembled at last! Note the wing and horizontal stabilizer components of the other aircraft at the bottom of the photograph (2 August 1925).
Schur Family and U.S. Navy

2 August. The wings were uncrated aboard the *Peary* and floated ashore on a raft made of two of the *Peary*'s dories lashed together and surfaced with the sides of the plywood wing crates. In the meantime, a work party had been prying the larger rocks and boulders out of the gravel beach. The remaining wing crates were disassembled aboard the *Peary*, floated ashore, and reassembled as a ramp running from the shore to the top of the beach. Beginning with NA-2, Lieutenant Schur's plane, the fuselages were lowered off the rear deck of the *Peary* and floated to the beach strapped between outriggers made from the dories. This was a very difficult operation, since the fuselages were inherently unstable without their wings and could over-turn and sink very easily. Once onshore, each fuselage was hauled up to the top of the beach tail-first by a party that included most of the members of the expedition and some of the local Inuhuit population. Each wing assembly

was then bolted in place while balanced on the backs of the crew. After each plane was assembled, it was floated out in the harbor and moored. The private papers of these hardy men do not even remark on the hazards of performing this difficult work in thirty-degree seawater. Schur, for example, would eventually lose four toes to a combination of the frigid water and open cockpit Arctic flying.

After NA-2 had been transported to the beach, Byrd notified the secretary of the navy of the operation's progress:

> Naval Unit started building runway for planes this morning at 5:30. Runway completed at 3 P.M. . . .
>
> Received much volunteer assistance today from civilian personnel of *Peary* and *Bowdoin* and some Eskimos . . . Took pigeons and pigeon house ashore tonight for training purposes . . .[1] Temperature this morning was around freezing. This afternoon it was drizzling and overcast. *Peary* and *Bowdoin* anchored about two hundred yards from shore.

Although many important scientific experiments and observations were made over the three-week stay at Etah, the major focus for most of the personnel was on the planes. The success of the air mission depended heavily on the weather, which had already demonstrated how variable and hazardous it could be. Like the Labrador coast, the northwest coast of Greenland had experienced the coldest spring in living memory and would have no real "summer season."

First Test Flights, 3–7 August

Late on 3 August, Lieutenant Schur took NA-2, the first Loening assembled, for a thirty-minute test flight. Rocheville, as mechanic, and Lieutenant Commander MacMillan, as observer, accompanied him. They flew out across Smith Sound and then returned to the Greenland coast to venture over the great ice cap for a brief time. Thus, Lt. (j.g.) M. A. Schur, USN, became the first American pilot to fly in the Far North and the first person in the world to overfly the ice cap of Greenland.

The next day, 4 August, Byrd and Bennett (NA-1) and Reber, Nold, and

3 August 1925. In-you-gee-to appears to stand pensively on the rocky Etah shore as Lieutenant Schur, MacMillan, and Rocheville taxi NA-2 out to change his world forever.

Schur Family Papers

First flight, 3 August 1925.
Schur Family and U.S. Navy

Sorensen (NA-3) took the other two planes on a slightly longer test hop and confirmed the observations of Schur and MacMillan. These two flights shattered some long-held views of the practicality of flying the polar seas in small aircraft of limited range.

The Inuhuit remained themselves, even as they observed with seeming equanimity the dawning of the age of polar flight and wireless communication in their midst. As Byrd observed in penciled notes on his personal copy of the final report to the navy recording the historic flight: "When Lt. Schur took the first flight at Etah, all the inhabitants of [the] small village collected in one *tupik* [tent] because, should the plane fall in the village, they wanted to die together."

The navy flyers had planned to land in emergencies on open areas of water or on suitably flat areas on the ice floes. The coldest winter and spring on record had reduced to practically nil the usually extensive areas of open water near Etah. Further, everyone had badly underestimated the extent of the pressure ridges in the seaborne ice fields. The specially fabricated skis for the Loenings would prove useless when faced with the often thirty-foot-high pressure ridges of ice. It was obvious to all during flights away from the clear water of Etah's Foulke Fjord that any serious difficulty with the untried inverted Liberty engines or with the airframe itself would mean certain death for the flyers involved.

Byrd's reaction to his and the world's first aerial view of these edges of the Polar Sea was published by *National Geographic*:

After passing Cape Sabine, the view that opened was magnificent, and we were stirred with the spirit of great adventure—with the feeling that we were getting a comprehensive idea, never before possible, of the Arctic's ruggedness and ruthlessness. I believe that we have a new story to tell of the grandeur of Ellesmere Island. It was evident that the greater part of the land we saw had been inaccessible to the foot traveler, who, keeping largely to the water routes, with the view cut off by the fjord's great perpendicular cliffs, could not have realized the colossal and multifold character of the glacier-cut mountains.

But there was no time to enjoy the view. Any slight engine trouble might require a landing, so I naturally looked about for some suitable place to which to put a plane down if necessary. The landing would have to be made flying at 40 or 50 miles an hour. I searched carefully and did not see a single place on the land or on the water where a landing would not have meant disaster. The land was everywhere too irregular and the water was filled with ice either broken up into drifting pieces or in large, unbroken areas. At that moment I realized we were confronted with an even more difficult and hazardous undertaking than we had anticipated. I knew, too, that no matter what judgment we exercised we would have to have a little luck to comply with Secretary Wilbur's last admonition to me to bring the personnel back safely. The Secretary had taken a great personal interest in the Expedition.

Commander MacMillan had confidently believed that the fjord would be free of ice. That it was not was due probably to the fact that we were having scarcely any summer.[2]

In an undated air operations report to the National Geographic Society, Byrd elaborated on his first flying experience over the Arctic and provided an insight to the dangers always facing the aviators:

> A good landing place while flying up there in the Arctic is certainly more welcome to the flyer than an oasis could be in the desert and this year they certainly are as scarce.
>
> Just then Bennett signaled me for the log book (you know you can't make yourself heard behind a Liberty motor) and wrote across a page: "Will you fly for a few minutes?"
>
> As I took the stick thinking that I was just taking my turn to fly, Bennett climbed out on the wing in that cold stream of air, and I knew that something was wrong with the engine, and I began to look around for a landing place, but there was nothing but jagged and snow covered mountains and cliffs and water full of rough ice so that a forced landing would have been a complete washout.
>
> I saw Bennett tinkering with the oil tank on the starboard fuselage. I knew then from the gauge that the tank was threatened with bursting from excessive oil pressure from some effect of the cold or some other cause. Bennett finally got the cap off the oil tank and that relieved the oil pressure.
>
> That was quick and courageous action typical of the officers and the men that the Navy sent with me.

The fifth of August was spent making short flights for radio tests, including testing the longwave radio transmitter from the USS *Florida* and checking the compasses. The planes were also subjected to a full load test to determine the effects of water and atmospheric conditions on their performance. It was determined that a maximum total weight for takeoff from the water was 5,500 pounds, which included the plane and engine weight of 3,600 pounds.[3] During these short flights, NA-2 had to make a forced landing due to water pump failure. The difficulty of navigating in the Arctic became obvious to the aviators during these short flights, as reported by Byrd to the secretary of the navy:

> Have calculated the variation of the compass here to be one hundred and three and one half degrees but the sun has been out for only about two or

three hours since we reached here, and I can not be certain of this variation. The intensity of the horizontal component of the earth's magnetism is so small here that the magnetic compass is practically useless in aircraft. The steering compass in NA-3 indicated east for all headings of the plane. Will test out earth induction compass tomorrow. Have had no chance to test sun compass due to cloudy weather.[4] Eskimos have been very apprehensive for the aviators as they do not see how the plane stays in the air and so fear that it will fall any minute.

Byrd's 6 August report to the Navy Department suggested the severe conditions and situations the unit was facing in preparing for the establishment of the forward base:

> Spent the morning and afternoon preparing for a consumption and radio and speed test for NA-2 and NA-3 with the food material, etc. we expect to take to first base. Both planes attempted to take off at 6 P.M., but it was found that with the material stowed in the tail of the plane the only available storage place the plane would not take off the water. At seven it began to rain with a steady downpour so had to cease flight operations. Have decided to remove 33 gallon gasoline tank, which is forward in the hull, and stow material there to balance plane better and enable us to get off the water with necessary load. Expect to have this finished tomorrow by 1 P.M. Sometime tomorrow afternoon NA-2 and NA-3 will make a reconnaissance flight towards Ellesmere Land to investigate landing conditions. Within the next two days hope to select a suitable place for landing our first base. Engine on NA-1 failed last night at 11 P.M. while on test flight necessitating changing engine which was done with the ships boom. The mechanics are now working on this engine and will have it ready for test tomorrow. The men with me are tireless in order to cope with the necessarily adverse operating conditions seldom knocking off work until near midnight. It seems best to get the motors well tuned in and conditioned before attempting a long flight . . .

Rain and gales prevented flying on 7 August and the crew worked on readying the planes for transporting materials to the forward base. The thirty-three-gallon forward gasoline tank was removed, allowing redistribution of cargo and solving the tail-heavy problem. The written record does not make more than a cursory comment about the removal of this fuel tank; however, doing so significantly shortened the operational radius of the Loenings and the margin of safety for long-range flight operations. Using Byrd's own figures from actual air operations at Etah, eighty miles per hour and twenty-three gallons per hour, removing the forward fuel tanks meant a loss of almost ninety minutes of flying time or 115 miles of range. The expedition was paying a high price for not being able to undertake balance and load tests prior to its departure.

During a squall, the NA-3 dragged anchor but the crew managed to get her safely tied up astern of the *Peary*. Changing the moorage would cause near disaster a short time later.

Aerial Exploration Begins, 8–11 August

Disaster was again narrowly avoided on 8 August when a gale blew a small iceberg into NA-3, fortunately causing no damage. This unexpected incursion of icebergs was probably a function of the unusually cold winter and spring that year in the North. The bergs were a constant hazard throughout the expedition's stay at Etah and forced the men to keep a twenty-four-hour iceberg watch in fair weather or foul.

Byrd and Bennett in NA-1 made a reconnaissance flight to Cape Sabine and Cape Isabella at 4:00 P.M. after a snowy and blustery morning. They reported a solid field of ice, with a few water leads, covering Smith Sound. NA-1 returned at eight o'clock and NA-2 and NA-3 were given orders to prepare for a flight to locate a base in Ellesmere Land. Byrd loaded a month's supply of food, a rifle, ammunition, a sleeping bag, a rubber boat, and a tent in NA-1 for deposition at the forward base.

NA-3, with Reber and Byrd, and NA-2, with Schur and Rocheville, left Etah at 9:10 P.M. for Cannon Fjord and the location of the forward base. Byrd's report to the navy about the 8–9 August flight clearly indicates the uniqueness and some of the hazards of flying in the Arctic:

> At 120 miles from Etah fog began to settle ahead and too thick to see through so it was decided to return to Etah. Had to fly at altitude of 3,800 feet to get above low clouds until we reached sight of Sound. Indicator showed 30-mile

gale blowing from the north, and water in harbor was quite rough whe[n] plane landed alongside *Peary* at five minutes before midnight . . .

Personnel got quite cold during flight and will put on more clothes for next flight. Eskimo clothes found to be the warmest. At mouth of harbor when NA-3 started to take off a huge herd of walrus came near the plane and appeared to get enraged at it, but they soon were left behind when we took off. A piece of ice weighing about 500 tons was blown by the gale into the harbor last night at 3 A.M., and it drifted between the *Peary* and the planes which were anchored hundred yards towards the shore from the ship. It is necessary to keep all night watch on the planes on account of the drifting ice.

Aerographer Francis has just handed me a report that a gale of great intensity is driving towards Etah from the Sound. All planes have been secured. As soon as the weather clears all three planes will make flight to the southern shore of the Bay Fjord in Ellesmere Land, 730 statute miles from Etah where Cdr. MacMillan says there is a landing field suitable for planes.

Based on this flight, Byrd further reported:

This flight of the 9th indicated that flying conditions over the fjords and rugged mantels and cliffs towards Cape Thomas Hubbard were very bad.

(a) There were no landing places on the land and an engine stopping over the land would have resulted in a tragedy.

(b) A large percentage of the jagged cliffs and rugged mountains were covered with mist.

(c) The mountains beyond Sawyer Bay (which lay on the course to Cape Thomas Hubbard) appeared higher and more numerous than was indicated by the chart and the Peaks were covered with clouds making their crossing with a heavily loaded plane very difficult if not impossible.

(d) There were very few areas in the ice covered fjords large enough to land in, and the ice was very evidently of a drifting nature and would close in and open up with wind or tide.

Weather and mechanical conditions were so much more hazardous than expected that Lieutenant Commander Byrd called a meeting of the air crews and told them that, though he personally would continue with air operations, all others were excused and would fly only as true volunteers. It is a great credit to all concerned that air operations were continued with all hands and, though they did not reach all of their original goals, they accomplished a great deal of valuable research.

Byrd's 10 August report to the secretary of the navy showed his frustration with the delays caused by the weather conditions:

> Weather continues bad and both Cdr. MacMillan and Aerographer Francis advised strongly against making a flight to Bay Fjord in Ellesmere Land until the low clouds and fog lift off the ground and mountains. No landing place could be found nor could a landing be made with fog covering the valleys. NA-1 and NA-3 made a radio test flight to Ellesmere Land at 5:30 P.M. Ran into snow over Cape Sabine. Got over the snow clouds and beyond could see no rift in clouds and fog that hung low over the mountains. Returned to ship at 7 P.M. The naval personnel is extremely anxious to make the first base, but they all realize that we are not warranted in trying to locate a landing field for a base with fog covering everything. The only thing therefore to do is to wait for the bad weather to break and then start immediately for Bay Fjord. It has snowed here several times today.

Based on the aviators' observations and reports, MacMillan, using his extensive knowledge of the Arctic, drafted an emergency plan in case of forced landing and forwarded it to Byrd on 10 August:

> I would suggest in the eventuality of a forced landing and damaged plane at any point beyond Cape Sabine that our line of retreat be as follows: By airboat southward through Eureka Sound following the west side to Storen Island where there is plenty of Musk oxen. Thence up the south side of the Bay Fjord to mouth of river and on by way of river valley to head of Flagler Fjord, where Arctic hare can be found by following south side to islands at mouth which are the breeding grounds of Eider duck and Glaucous gulls. From there a direct course can be taken to Outer Island from the Thorvald Pa. [Peninsula] and on to Shroelling Island. Here the boat should follow closely along shore to Cape Rutherford and on down through Rice Strait to the house at which point they can be rescued by plane or boat.

The storm cleared sufficiently by midday, 11 August, and the push toward a forward base resumed. All three planes were off at 10:40 A.M., headed as far toward Axel Heiberg Land as possible, in an attempt to discover a protected ice-free fjord in which to establish the base. Byrd's official report to the Navy Department made clear the difficulty of this flight:

Left Etah this morning at ten-forty for the purpose of locating a landing place to form a base between Etah and the polar sea. This base is absolutely necessary as fuel and feed must be deposited on shore of polar sea before a flight can be made out over polar sea. Passed over northwest end of Cape Sabine at eleven-fifteen. Reached eastern end of Flagler Fjord at eleven forty-five. Altitude of NA-1 seven thousand feet, NA-2 and NA-3 about four thousand feet. Reached western end of Flagler Fjord at twelve-[oh]-seven P.M. Temperature bitterly cold several degrees below zero at seventy-three hundred feet. Hundreds of mountain peaks to left all covered with dazzling white snow, and clouds covering everything to right with mountains much higher than shown on chart as at altitude of seventy-three hundred feet some of the mountains most of which are shown at all on maps were hundreds of feet higher than plane. Saw much land probably never seen before. At twelve-[oh]-seven set course to two hundred and fifty degrees true, which made compass course approximately twelve degrees. Checked magnetic compass with sun compass and found that magnetic compass had thirty degrees westerly deviation which put compass one hundred and seventy degrees off the true course. Sun compass very good when sun is visible. Hit the eastern end of Bay Fjord at twelve forty-five P.M. The fjord was largely obscured by clouds. This part of the fjord that could be seen was almost entirely covered with ice. At twelve forty-eight NA-2 disappeared in clouds to the right, and NA-3 which was having difficulty getting altitude turned back towards Etah. NA-1 continued to Eureka Sound southwest of Axel Heiberg Land two hundred miles from Etah and found only one suitable landing place which was on the northern shore of Bay Fjord in approximately longitude eighty-five. NA-1 returned to search for other planes, but clouds had closed in behind and had to fly over them. Set course for Beitstad Fjord and found it free of clouds and also ice. Approximately one hundred miles from Etah. NA-2 and NA-3 reached Etah at two-thirty P.M. and NA-1 at three-fifteen. Reber reported that he suffered slightly from snow blindness. All personnel suffered from cold. Must take advantage of this good weather so three planes will start tonight at 9 P.M. to establish a sub base at western end of Beitstad Fjord. Will leave there food cooking, utensils, primus stove, rifle and ammunition and gasoline and oil . . . Distances are given in statute miles.

In later years, Lieutenant Commander Byrd spoke of this flight as the most hazardous of the expedition. He spoke of the frustration of not having adequate navigation instruments and, on this flight, of sighting over the tailfin of the Loening to known geographical features they had flown past to gain a crude measure of the amount of wind drift! He also mentioned that such sightings to the rear on the outbound leg of the flight helped the aviators find their way on the return journey to Etah.

At 9:30 P.M. all three planes were back in the air. The crews were the same except Commander McDonald replaced Nold in NA-3 and Rocheville replaced Commander MacMillan in NA-2. Thirty minutes into the flight, NA-2 left the loose formation, forced back to Etah with "low temperature in the motor." The remaining two planes reached Beitstad Fjord (which was stunningly beautiful by all accounts), but they could not land due to a severe cross wind over the restricted open water of the fjord. Both planes returned to Etah by midnight.

Storms Intervene, 12–13 August

The planes were grounded all of the next day, due to yet another gale. The following day was even worse. Byrd recorded this difficult day in his official activities report to the secretary of the navy:

> Everything seemed to go wrong on the 13th. During the night hours it got quite rough and a very difficult time was experienced with the NA-3 astern of the *Peary.* Her lower wings were slightly injured by collision with the barrel raft (used for working on planes) when it broke loose from its mooring astern the *Peary.* The plane was saved from more severe injury by prompt action of Nold. The NA-1 and NA-3 also were threatened by the drifting ice several times so that the Navy personnel got very little rest.
>
> Bennett and Sorensen, while working on motor of the NA-1 in rough water, lost the starboard cowling overboard. This is a large hinged sheet of duralumin and difficult to make. Bennett and Sorensen took a plain sheet of "dural" and worked all night on the deck in the cold making a new cowling. The work was finished about six A.M., and Bennett and Sorensen reported

for a day's work—did not want to turn in but wanted to go on with a scheduled flight.

This is the kind of superhuman work effort the personnel with me had been making. This cowling had to be riveted and catches made so as to fit snugly on the plane before she could fly.

The continual pounding of the waves opened up a seam in the NA-2 (which was tied up astern of the *Bowdoin*) early in the morning. She began to go down by the nose. She went down until the motor was three quarters submerged, and it was with the greatest difficulty and hard labor on the part of all hands on the *Bowdoin* that she was saved from destruction. She was finally hoisted aboard the *Peary* in order to shift motors and repair the bottom. Unfortunately she was further damaged by the Mates accidentally letting her down on the deck so hard that the keel was injured.

Attempts to Establish Forward Bases, 14–16 August

On 14 August, using NA-1 and NA-3, the aviators were at last able to establish their first forward base cache at the west end of Flagler Fjord, about 150 miles west-northwest of Etah. On 14 August Byrd sent this radiogram to the secretary of the navy:

> At eleven forty-five this morning NA-3 (Schur and Sorensen) NA-1 (Bennett and Byrd) left Etah for western end of Flagler Fjord one hundred and seven miles from Etah. Reached objective at 1:15 and found at last place to land in water. Got planes fifty yards from beach and waded ashore with supplies. Deposited one hundred yards from beach two hundred pounds of food and one hundred gallons of gasoline, five gallons oil, primus stove, camping outfit, smoke bombs, rifle and ammunition, one gallon kerosene and can of matches. At 3:00 P.M. large block of ice drifted into NA-1 but after half hour got her clear of ice. Wind carries ice with great force. Left Flagler Fjord at 3:35 P.M. and reached Etah at 5:10 P.M. Flagler Fjord is like a magnificent glacier. Its walls rise over two thousand feet up from the Fjord. The magnificence and ruggedness of the country flown over is indescribable. Bennett and Sorensen worked all night to make a cowling for the left side of the motor of the NA-1. Her cowling blew overboard in the gale yesterday. NA-2 is on deck of the *Peary* having her motor shifted and bottom repaired. In order to take

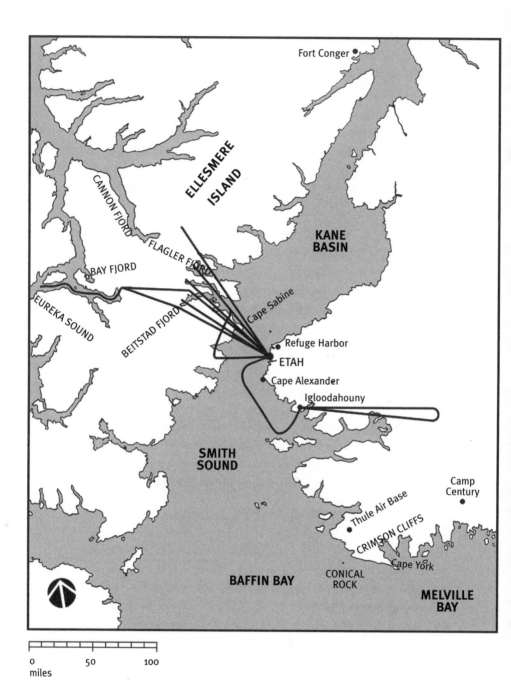

Fort Conger

ELLESMERE ISLAND

CANNON FJORD

FLAGLER FJORD

BAY FJORD

EUREKA SOUND

BEITSTAD FJORD

KANE BASIN

Cape Sabine

Refuge Harbor

ETAH

Cape Alexander

Igloodahouny

SMITH SOUND

Camp Century

Thule Air Base

CRIMSON CLIFFS

Cape York

BAFFIN BAY

CONICAL ROCK

MELVILLE BAY

0   50   100
miles

FLIGHTS BY THE NAVAL ARCTIC UNIT, 3–23 AUGUST 1925
John H. Bryant, FAIA

Lieutenant Commander Byrd poses with partly disassembled NA-2 in background, August 1925. His "all-Eskimo" flying outfit was much superior to the
navy's standard cold-weather issue.
Schur Family Papers

All three Loenings often were moored close aboard the *Peary*. Here, NA-2 is attached to the winch to be lifted aboard for major repairs. In the midground, mechanics are performing work on the Liberty engine of the second Loening while supporting themselves on a raft made from one of the wing crate sides and four empty fuel barrels. Note, also, the iceberg floating ominously close to the third Loening in the background.

Schur Family and U.S. Navy

advantage of fair weather, as soon as planes can take on gasoline will leave for base and deposit gasoline and oil. NA-3 Nold pilot NA-1 Bennett and Byrd. Taking only one pilot in NA-3 in order to be able to carry more fuel.

On 15 August the two planes returned to Flagler Fjord with additional supplies and gasoline. Byrd reported to the Navy Department:

> After establishing a base yesterday at the end of Flagler Fjord, NA-1 and NA-3 left at nine[-oh-] five P.M. to leave additional hundred and sixty gallons of gasoline at base, but tide and wind had filled water with ice and landing was impossible. No proper landing place was found anywhere near this base so planes returned to *Peary* arriving at twelve-thirty P.M. NA-3 (Schur and Sorensen) and NA-1 (Byrd and Bennett) leaving tonight 10 P.M. for Cannon Fjord in Ellesmere Land to deposit food and gasoline.

The air crews returned to base very disappointed and NA-3 was stood down for needed repairs.

At 10:45 P.M. on the sixteenth, the indefatigable aviators were back up in NA-1 (Byrd, Bennett) and NA-3 (Schur, Sorensen) to ferry supplies to a new cache location farther to the west at Cannon Fjord. At midnight, about 105 miles from base, they found the mountains covered with fog so thick that it was impossible to continue over or through them. They noted that Flagler Fjord was still ice-packed, but they found some open water in Sawyer Bay and landed for a midnight lunch on the partially open beach. The weather cleared at 4:15 A.M. and both planes took off. Schur (NA-3) had to land almost immediately due to a knock in the engine. Byrd and Bennett continued on with one last attempt to reach Cannon Fjord. Byrd's report to the navy spoke of the ruggedness of the conditions as well as the great beauty of the region:

> At altitude of 5,000 feet cleared mountains shown on chart at 5:20 and got over unexplored regions of Grinnell Land. Found high uncharted mountains entirely covered with snow. Saw many square miles never before seen by man. There was an uncharted lake frozen over. The jaggedness, irregularity and many deep valleys presented a magnificent but awful spectacle. The air was the roughest ever experienced by us. At five thirty reached high peaks that were completely covered with clouds. Made effort to get through but it was impossible. Returned to Sawyer Bay reaching there at 6 A.M. and planes

deposited one hundred gallons of gasoline five gallons oil and some pemmi-can. NA-3 and NA-1 started return trip at 7:05. Ran into fifty-mile gale over Smith Sound and reached Etah at 8:30. Had difficulty tying up to ships due to rough water. It has been blowing a gale all day and snowed from nine to ten P.M.

Both planes returned to Etah safely, despite the ever increasing knock in the engine of NA-3.

Gales Ground Aircraft, 17–20 August

The gale blew all day on the seventeenth and most of the eighteenth. During that time, and under very difficult working conditions, the engine on NA-3 was changed out; the engine knock Schur had noted proved to be a failing rod bearing. Disaster nearly struck the aviators again on 17 August when aviation gasoline leaked from barrels aboard the *Peary* and formed an unnoticed slick aft. Byrd described the incident in his final report:

> On the 17th the gale finally subsided. At 8:00 P.M. gasoline on the water around the *Peary* caught fire, and for a few moments it looked as if the NA-3, which was tied up astern, and the whole ship would go. Sorensen and Rocheville used splendid head work in casting the NA-3 adrift immediately, and Lt. Schur showed great calmness and judgement in procuring a pyrene [fire extinguisher] immediately and throwing it to Nold who was on the flaming plane. Lt. Schur threw the pyrene very carefully steadying Nold as he prepared to throw it. If the pyrene had been missed the plane would have been lost. Nold showed very commendable courage to stick to his post with the plane ablaze . . . The saving of NA-3 from destruction by fire today was just another example of the fine spirit of the personnel the Navy has assigned to me for this duty. Whether we succeed or fail they deserve the highest success. They have overcome almost insuperable odds that the elements and poor facilities have brought about. They have been indefatigable and courageous, and whenever there has been a job to do they have needed no commanding officer to tell them to do it to spur them to greater effort. What they have accomplished on this trip has been almost superhuman and even if we do not succeed in the highest measure it could hardly overcome my pride in

them. Their attitude seems to have been to live up to the best tradition of the Navy.

That day, MacMillan informed Byrd that he had decided to wait one more week at Etah for the aviators to attempt completion of their work. He added, "If, at the end of that time, you and the men under your command believe that, given three day[s] more, the Expedition can reach a point on the Polar Sea at least two hundred miles west from any part of Axel Heiberg Land, I will gladly remain."

Sometime the next day, however, Commander MacMillan made a preliminary decision to curtail operations and begin the return journey on or before the scheduled departure date of 21 August. On 20 August he sent the following message to Byrd:

> I have received a long radiogram from the National Geographic Society since talking with you yesterday. I have talked to the majority of your men who declare that it will be impossible for us to carry out plans. Last night the head of Etah Fjord froze over as it did the night before. A forced landing in Cannon Fjord or Eureka Sound would certainly result in a freezing in of the plane and a detention of the Bowdoin for fifteen months.
>
> In view of the fact that all other work as planned by the National Geographic is being prevented by our delay I have decided to prepare for home at once.
>
> I would suggest that NA-2 and NA-3 be placed on board at once that NA-1 fly over the ice cap to Igloodahounay. If you would like to take the trip you can depend on Schur for a knowledge of the location of the place where there is a good sand beach.

At the same time, MacMillan sent a long radiogram to the National Geographic Society in which he made clear his concern that the expedition could be trapped if it did not leave before the end of the short summer. He also voiced his disappointment with the airplanes' ability to perform the exploratory work. MacMillan concluded:

> I am more confirmed than ever that far northern Arctic work will never be done by heavier than air machines simply because landing places are

uncertain and caches of food and gas cannot be depended upon. A fjord is free today and ice bound tomorrow. A cache under such conditions is not a help but a menace for if depended upon and a plane arrives out of fuel, destruction is the inevitable result.

Byrd protested vigorously the decision to leave, wishing to delay the departure and arguing that the Naval Aviation Unit needed only three or four days of good flying weather to complete its mission:

I was very much delighted yesterday when you decided to let us continue our efforts to accomplish our mission because I believe we have a chance to succeed. I have just received your letter stating that we must prepare to go home at once. I am distressed beyond measure that we won't try again for the polar sea, and I beg you to reconsider your decision. Of course I realize that you are using your best judgement and grant that it may be better than mine, only I feel that we still have a chance to succeed. I would like to take that chance. Today is the 20th, and I think with four or five good days we could get out over the polar sea by using relief pilots.

. . . I of course, unhesitatingly obey your order to pack up and go home early only I feel it my duty to express my true feelings to you.

Byrd also disagreed with MacMillan's conclusion that heavier-than-air craft were unsuited to Arctic exploration and stated so, officially, in his Official Activities Report.

Radiograms shot back and forth between Etah and Washington for the next twenty-four hours. Byrd attempted to send a coded message to the Navy Department, the first coded message of the trip. McDonald refused to send it, telling Byrd:

I have carefully considered the contents of your cipher message as you decoded it to me, and I can see no reason why it should not go in plain English as there is nothing in it of a confidential nature and none of the messages up to the present time sent from the *Peary* or the *Bowdoin* have to my knowledge been used by any other than the addressee. I will be very glad to transmit anything you have to say to the Navy Department if written in plain English.

The flow of messages culminated with Secretary Wilbur's message to the expedition stating that the Navy Department considered "further attempts to fly over polar sea not advisable this season" and ordering it to withdraw. He praised the expedition's efforts: "Department highly appreciates the fine spirit and splendid work of the Naval Unit under your command under very severe weather conditions."

Radio from the Top of the World

Radio activity was particularly dense during the three weeks at Etah. The two main tasks for the three radio operators were standing radio watches in support of flight operations and arranging a series of broadcasts featuring the Inuhuit of Smith Sound. The first of several broadcasts was arranged when WAP (the *Peary*) notified Zenith, the press, and the amateur radio community that the first broadcast from the Far North would take place on Saturday night, 1 August. The notice was sent out on Thursday, 30 July, from WAP. A 15 August article in the then-prominent trade publication, *The Talking Machine World,* detailed the first two of these broadcasts as follows:

> The press of the country and the higher powered broadcasting stations notified the public of the amazing event, and at the appointed time both amateurs and the Zenith experimental station 9XN with its two operators stood by and waited.[5] WAP sent out their CQ call, signaling their going on the air, and faintly came the voices of McDonald and MacMillan, gradually increasing in volume, until, within one-half hour, the Arctic voices were as clear and distinguishable as continental stations. Music and songs were reproduced with such faithfulness as to make even the hardened operators stand aghast. Radio had penetrated the Auroral bands, a feat heretofore never accomplished during the six months of Arctic daylight.

On Sunday, McDonald radioed the Zenith offices that reports of reception had been heard not only in various parts of the U.S., but in London as well. McDonald was so excited that his predictions about shortwave in the Arctic were accurate that he announced that he and MacMillan would submit to a "real time" press conference via radio on the following evening, 3 August, at

11:30 P.M. That evening, various Zenith officials, guests, representatives of Chicago newspapers, and the Associated Press gathered at the little transmitter shack of Zenith's experimental radio station, 9XN, in Arlington Heights, some forty miles from the Loop. S. I. Marks, then general manager of Zenith and McDonald's normal contact at headquarters during this trip, briefed the guests on the procedure for the press conference. Each reporter was asked to draft a single question. These were then sent to McDonald and MacMillan, apparently via Morse code rather than by voice. In all, five questions were sent to WAP during the press conference and the answers came back very rapidly. The press conference was so successful that other messages were exchanged that evening that resulted in McDonald's promise to broadcast a program of Eskimo music from WAP to 9XN. The program was to then be relayed live to the country on the AM broadcast band by WJAZ. The broadcast was to occur "within the next thirty days."

For Zenith and most radio fans, the most memorable radio events of the 1925 expedition were the next two radio broadcasts made from the *Peary* during that three weeks at anchor in Foulke Fjord. The first occurred on the evening of 12 August and was noted in MacMillan's diary as "our Broadcast to America." According to a list MacMillan made, the program included:

1. Accordion played by Bromfield and Gayer.
2. Music of the Eskimo by myself [MacMillan].
3. General introduction and remarks by McDonald.
4. Singing by Eskimos and beating of Kilante via Eskimo drum.

The second broadcast was heard aboard the USS *Seattle,* then at anchor in the harbor at Wellington, New Zealand. This broadcast was described in MacMillan's biography by Allen and was referred to several times in reports to the National Geographic Society. It was also mentioned on many occasions in personal letters between MacMillan and McDonald and between McDonald and high-ranking navy officials. Admiral MacMillan also discussed the broadcast in detail in a 1955 nationwide television program, *Omnibus.* Unfortunately, none of these sources gives the exact date of the broadcast, although evidence suggests that it was made sometime between

McDonald (seated) hosted several shortwave radio broadcasts "From the Top of the World" that featured Inuhuit singing. MacMillan, standing to McDonald's right, and Schur (right background) observe the proceedings, August 1925. The round object on the table is an early microphone.
Zenith

16 August and 19 August, most likely 19 August. This broadcast was described in the most detail, though somewhat inaccurately, in the June 1943 issue of Zenith's internal newsmagazine, *Zenith Radio Log:*

> On an August day in 1925 six Eskimos from the world's most northerly settlement gathered before a microphone on the s.s. *Peary* as she lay at anchor near Etah, Greenland, less than 700 miles from the North Pole. They sang some of their song for Admiral Coontz of the United States Fleet, which was cruising off the shores of Tasmania [*sic*], south of Australia, half the world away.
>
> "That's not singing," exclaimed the Admiral. "It sounds like a college yell to me." "Perfect!" exulted Commander McDonald, president of Zenith. "That's what Eskimo songs sound like. It proves that our transmission is getting through to you okay."

From his icy anchorage in northern Greenland, our skipper had sent the human voice halfway round the world, and demonstrated once and for all that short-wave radio was the answer to our navy's need for dependable long-distance communication.

Earlier in the year, Commander McDonald had persuaded Admiral [sic] Ridley McLean, director of naval communications, to commission a young amateur named Fred Schnell as a lieutenant in the navy, and assign him to the Seattle, flagship of the fleet, to experiment with short-wave. Schnell sailed away with the fleet, smarting at first under the derision which some officers directed toward his "pin box radio." Soon, however, he began startling fleet communication officers by keeping direct contact with other amateurs in the United States long after the fleet was so far from land that it was beyond the range of its regular long-wave radio.

In fact, there was a heavy volume of communications between the Peary at Etah and stations Down Under during the expedition's three-week stay at Foulke Fjord. Schnell reported at the time that the signal from the Peary's transmitter was almost always significantly stronger in Wellington than that of station 9XN in Chicago. McDonald summarized the most important aspects of the expedition's radio activities in similar messages to National Geographic and to The Talking Machine World:

> We consistently maintained communication not only with the United States, but with England, Scotland, France, Holland, Italy, Hawaii, New Zealand, and Australia, the greatest distance having been a two-way communication with Box Hill, Victoria, Australia, nearly halfway around the earth on 37.5 meters. We transmitted the voices of the Eskimo singing his primitive songs within 11.5 degrees of the North Pole, and these songs were heard in Australia and New Zealand, and we received an official radiogram of congratulations both from the Governor-General of New Zealand and the Governor General of Australia. Lieutenant Fred Schnell, with his short-wave apparatus on the u.s.s. Seattle, desiring to send a radiogram extending his compliments to the Convention of the American Radio Relay League [being] held in Chicago, on August 16, being unable to reach Chicago direct, was forced to send it from his ship laying off Wellington, New Zealand, to the MacMillan Arctic ss Peary, within 11.5 degrees of the North Pole, and we in turn relayed back to Chicago, consuming less than five minutes.

Along with their duties related to the air operations and to the broadcasts, Radio Operators Reinartz, aboard the *Bowdoin,* and McGee and Gray, aboard the *Peary,* continued to produce the daily "newspaper," composed of news releases from the United States and Nauen, Germany, that was so important to all hands, as well as to transmit regular reports to the National Geographic Society and the navy. They were also quite active in communicating with many radio amateurs from a number of countries.[6] One amateur, teenager Arthur Collins of Cedar Rapids, Iowa, received a great deal of publicity for being an important link between the *Bowdoin* and the outside world. Commander McDonald found time on 18 August to answer personal correspondence and to salute many of his close friends "from the Top of the World." Many of the messages reveal how impressed McDonald was with the Etah area and how appreciative he was of friends' concerns for the safety of the expedition. This message to Capt. E. A. Evers of the uss *Commodore* is typical of many found in McDonald's files:

> My greetings to you and the officers of the *Commodore* from north of seventy-eight where the nights are six months long. Ask Sport for the rest of the words and you will get my meaning. I wish that you and your officers could be with me on this trip thru this fairyland of savage scenic grandeur where happiness and wonderful hunting surround you. Bucking the ice of the dreaded Melville Bay was truly and [*sic*] experience, all day, all night that cry sings out: Port—Starboard—Steady, as you worm thru the openings and splint the pans. The *Peary* is a wonderful ice bucker, and frankly the *Bowdoin* would never have come thru in so short a time had the *Peary* not broken the ice. Sorry I was forced to miss your dinner. May I have a rain check on my return?

Problems with the Relay of Radio Messages

The records of this expedition and the private papers of MacMillan and McDonald record that, during the expedition's stay at Etah, John L. Reinartz, radio operator on the *Bowdoin* and chief radio operator of the expedition, was demoted for cause; Paul McGee, first radio operator of the *Peary,* was made chief operator in his place. The reason for Reinartz's demotion was quite serious, but was intentionally left out of the official written record of the expedition by McDonald and MacMillan so as not to "ruin the boy's future." Still, the misbehavior was so serious that McDonald had his lawyer meet the *Peary* on its return to "explain his predicament" to Reinartz.

The reasons for this extraordinary occurrence were at least partly related to Reinartz's apparent failure to give proper attention to transmitting and receiving the expedition's official communications. Several pieces of correspondence over the years between McDonald and MacMillan and between McDonald and Schnell refer to Reinartz's failure to move official expedition communications. McDonald ascribed Reinartz's motives as his desire to impress and communicate with his amateur radio colleagues. This was one of the first "exotic location" radio expeditions. Thanks to the use of the new shortwave frequencies hams from throughout the world had for the first time in history the opportunity to contact a station (Reinartz) in such an exotic location. They would also then receive a coveted commemorative "QSL" card verifying their achievement. Commander McDonald's judgement is therefore most likely correct; the pressure on Reinartz must have been tremendous.

In reviewing the surviving official radiograms between the expedition and the National Geographic Society, the navy, and Zenith Radio Corporation, it is obvious that some messages that the expedition leaders thought had gone were not sent or, at least, they were never received, even though the authors had been told by Reinartz that receipt had been confirmed. It also seems clear, early in the voyage at least, that John Reinartz favored communications with his radio amateur brethren while ignoring schedules and calls from the navy stations. All of this caused a good deal of confusion and, at least late in the voyage, some obvious anger and hard feelings between the three expedition leaders and their supporters back in the U.S. It is easy to speculate that the apparently frosty relations between MacMillan and McDonald on one side and the National Geographic Society on the other, which seem to have developed during the expedition, had their genesis in the *Bowdoin*'s radio room.

The written record also indicates that the other radio operators on the expedition, McGee and Gray, along with McDonald, came to believe that Reinartz manipulated the circuits of the Zenith equipment on the *Peary* so that the electrical load of the transmitter burned up the generator armatures. This put the transmitter out of operation. In a 27 October 1925 letter to Capt. Ridley McLean, McDonald withdrew his April 1925 request for a navy commission for Reinartz, explaining:

> At Hopedale, Labrador, we had experienced so much difficulty that I ordered Reinartz aboard the *Peary* until the apparatus was in workable condition. He pronounced it, after one day's work, as workable at Hopedale, and I permitted him to go back on board the *Bowdoin*. One day out of Hopedale the apparatus again started burning up our generators. McGee and Gray conferred with me and frankly stated that they believed they were being deliberately misled and asked permission to redesign the apparatus. I granted this permission when we were down to our last armature—they rebuilt the apparatus, and from that point on, we experienced no further difficulty, as is evidenced by the consistent communication that we maintained.
>
> Both Commander MacMillan and myself are convinced that Reinartz did not want any radio apparatus to work except that which he was operating. There, however, up to this time, might have been a question as to whether Reinartz's acts were deliberate or because of lack of knowledge—however, when we reached Etah, Reinartz was at first unable to establish communication with civilization and each day the messages were sent over to the *Peary* for us to clear them. After two or three days of this performance Reinartz stated that he was clearing his messages, but we ascertained thru a check-up, merely accidental, that he was okaying for messages that were never transmitted or that were never received. It was then that I demoted him and placed Paul McGee in the position of Chief Operator of the MacMillan Expedition.
>
> . . . It may interest you also to know that Reinartz has persistently [mis]represented himself as a Lieutenant in the Naval Reserve Force.

In a private telegram to S. I. Marks at Zenith, who needed advice on what to tell the press, McDonald stated that Reinartz had lied about sending many messages. He advised Marks that the story was not for publication but could be repeated to the lawyer.

When one considers that one of the major goals of the expedition was to demonstrate the ability of shortwave radio to outperform the longwave radio equipment then in use, the grave implications of Reinartz's behavior are obvious. Not only might the replacement of longwave radio equipment with shortwave for navy fleet operations have been delayed, but the reputation of Zenith in this very public venture would also have suffered.

It is also interesting to note that McDonald's cordial relationship with amateur radio's ARRL and its officials continued unbroken. Apparently, President Maxim and the other ARRL officials felt the evidence against Reinartz was overwhelming. If even part of what the other operators and McDonald alleged actually happened, Reinartz's behavior was directly contrary to the ethical standards of the ARRL.

Storm's End: Flight Operations Resume

On 20 August, the burned wings of NA-3 were replaced, a spare Liberty engine was installed, and the aviators prepared to resume flight operations. After lengthy discussions, everyone agreed that the two remaining planes would make short photographic flights in the Etah area on the twentieth and twenty-first as the expedition packed up. Then, as the ships left on 22 August, the aviators would make one long flight out over the unexplored regions of the Greenland Ice Cap and meet the ships at Igloodahouny, an Eskimo encampment about fifty miles to the south.

The short photographic flights were successful and early on the 22 August, NA-1, with Byrd, Bennett, and Francis aboard, and NA-3, carrying Reber, Nold, and Gayer, took off and headed south for Igloodahouny, the jumping-off point for the ice cap. Half a mile from Etah, the engine of the NA-3 threw a connecting rod; the engine seized and stopped dead. Pilot Reber made an emergency landing and the plane had to be towed back to the harbor. NA-1 landed briefly to confirm the safety of NA-3, then continued on to Igloodahouny. After establishing a camp on the shore, Byrd, Bennett, and Francis flew out over the unexplored, uncharted northern Greenland Ice Cap. This single intrepid flight confirmed that the ice cap did, indeed, rise continually from the coast and that it appeared to crest in the center of the island at an altitude of over eleven thousand feet. They also noted that although the coastal regions of the ice cap were crevasse-ridden and unacceptable for landing, the interior appeared smooth, featureless, and capable of supporting aircraft. For the first time, Byrd noted that aerial exploration in the North was uncomfortable in the open cockpit of the unheated Loenings. He said that the crew was "frozen stiff" by the time the plane landed back at Igloodahouny.

The *Bowdoin* arrived at Igloodahouny ahead of the *Peary,* which had delayed to load the last equipment at Etah. The next morning MacMillan and Bennett set off on what was to be the last flight of the expedition. They flew south along the coast to Karna, the home of E-took-a-shoo, MacMillan's favorite sledging companion and chief assistant of past expeditions. According to Kennett Rawson:

> When E-took-a-shoo saw the plane come skimming along the land in front of his *tupik,* he was flabbergasted. But when the Commander invited him to fly back to Ig-loo-da-douny, he simply said, "Wait till I get my mittens." Then with utter confidence in his own safety while he was at the Commander's side, he mounted into this strange machine and flew back to Ig-loo-da-houny with as little concern as if he had been on his own sledge.

With NA-1's return to Igloodahouny, air operations were terminated. The *Peary* had arrived during the flight, and the crew, assisted by their Inuhuit friends, soon disassembled the last Loening and loaded it aboard for the trip home. Byrd's summary of the air mission at Etah showed that NA-1 had flown thirty-two hours and twenty-five minutes; NA-2 had flown twenty-seven hours and twenty-two minutes; and NA-3 had flown twenty-nine hours and thirty minutes.

FIVE

Southbound for Home

*W*HILE THE *PEARY* LOADED THE LAST LOENING Amphibian off the beach at Igloodahouny, the *Bowdoin* weighed anchor and turned south to Karna to return E-took-a-shoo to his family. The route lay through largely uncharted waters. MacMillan had noted a dotted line (usually indicating shoals) south of Igloodahouny and had inspected the area from the air on the flight up from Karna. There appeared to be no shoals so MacMillan and the *Bowdoin* rather casually set off down the coast.

MacMillan described what happened:

> We were going full speed about a mile off the beach when there came a tremendous crash, hard enough it seemed, to rip the whole bottom out of our staunch little ship and sounding especially violent to both Robinson and myself, who were down in the cabin donning oilskins in anticipation of a heavy rainstorm approaching from Inglefield Bay.
>
> We scrambled up the ladder to the afterdeck. One glance was sufficient. We were high and dry, as a sailor would say, and so high forward that I knew we would not come off until the next tide . . . The all-important question right then was, "What kind of a bottom are we on?" If on ragged rocks, the

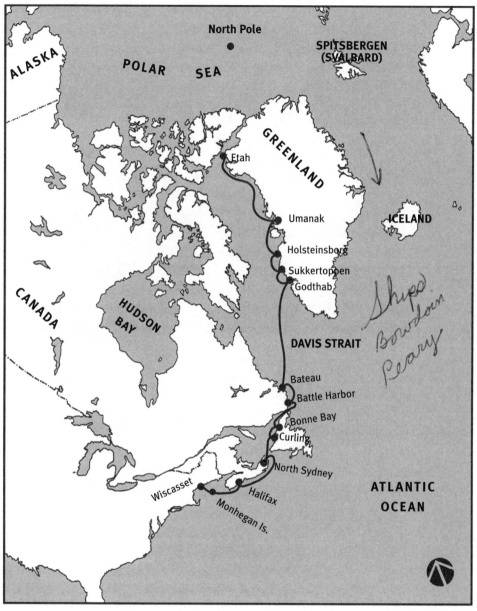

North Pole

SPITSBERGEN
(SVALBARD)

ALASKA

POLAR   SEA

GREENLAND

ICELAND

Etah

Umanak

Holsteinsborg

Sukkertoppen

Godthab

CANADA

HUDSON
BAY

DAVIS STRAIT

Ships
Bowdoin
Peary

Bateau

Battle Harbor

Bonne Bay

Curling

North Sydney

ATLANTIC
OCEAN

Wiscasset

Halifax

Monhegan Is.

0   250   500
miles

SOUTHBOUND FOR HOME
John H. Bryant, FAIA

Soon after embarking on the return voyage, Lieutenant Commander MacMillan ran the *Bowdoin* hard aground on a rocky reef near Igloodahouny. She suffered moderate damage to the keel, but she was refloated at the next high tide and proceeded south.
Schur Family Papers

Bowdoin with her heavy deck load of 39 barrels of gas, might suffer considerably in spite of her staunch construction of white oak, armored with ironwood and backed with cement . . .

To receive a serious injury to the hull of the *Bowdoin*, 3,000 miles from home, might place us in a predicament. It would relieve us of considerable anxiety to have the *Peary* standing by, in case we were in need of her help. She received our signals and rushed to our assistance.

Meanwhile the *Bowdoin* had listed so heavily to starboard and was so high on the rocks that we could walk under her prow and make an examination of the keel. We found the shoe almost completely gone, and the keel itself so badly split and splintered that we trimmed off large sections with an ax. But, knowing the thoroughness of her construction, we had no fears whatever as to her seaworthiness for the homeward trip.

To watch the incoming tide flow over her rail and up the slanting deck was no new experience. It had happened in 1923 and 1924. We knew that she would rise as she did, and within an hour we were afloat.[1]

With the *Bowdoin* once more afloat, the *Peary* headed south for Holsteinsborg, almost one thousand miles to the south. The *Bowdoin* made two brief stops as she followed the *Peary* down the Greenland coast. By all accounts, both vessels made a remarkably swift and uneventful run. MacMillan's "ice report" made to the Danish officials in Godthab noted that, though they were constantly surrounded by icebergs, the dreaded Melville Bay ice pack was not in evidence. MacMillan's diary on this segment of the voyage is full of references to the wonderful ease of voice communications between the two ships.

On the way south, the *Peary* had to shut off the steam radiators in the cabins and "run cold" because of the nearly depleted coal supply. She paused for the evening of 26 August at Umanak. No coal was loaded, but McDonald and the local inhabitants made one final two-hour-long broadcast of Eskimo music. Records indicate that this broadcast was heard in both Australia and New Zealand. It was also very well received in Chicago, where a special radio concert was arranged. Present at the concert were a number of Zenith executives and their wives, along with various Chicago dignitaries, including Mr. and Mrs. Frederick H. Rawson, whose son Kennett was the youngest member of the expedition crew. There were also several other members of the national and local press in attendance. *The Talking Machine World* covered the broadcast in some detail:

> Popular songs and Eskimo music broadcast from the MacMillan Arctic expedition, while it was anchored off Etah, Greenland [all expedition records indicate that the *Peary* was at anchor at Umanak rather than at Etah on this date], 3,700 miles away were heard by a thrilled audience of twenty-five people in the Zenith experimental station, 9XN, at Arlington Heights, Ill., on the evening of August 26.
>
> Both voice and instrumental selections were heard but the phonograph numbers were most clearly received. The reception marked the first time that an assembly has heard entertainment broadcast from the Arctic. The first selection was heard at 10:35 P.M., when the strains of "What'll I Do?" came

floating through 3,700 miles of space, followed soon after by "Marchetta." The Eskimos then took their places before the microphone, with various instruments made of bones and skins of wild animals, accompanied by their voices. Limited time curtailed the further broadcasting of their program.

Both Schur and Byrd wrote of a memorable incident that occurred that evening in the small island harbor. A large iceberg "calved" (split into two sections) with a thunderous roar and then rolled over. The water seemed to run out of the harbor and then returned with a rush. Everyone ran from the beach in a panic to escape the oncoming tidal wave, but one small child was caught and carried back into the deep icy water. Lieutenant Schur was able to use the *Peary*'s small boat to rescue the child from certain death and take her to a nearby Danish vessel for first aid. The next morning, the *Peary* proceeded south to meet the *Bowdoin* in Holsteinsborg.

Holsteinsborg

The faster *Peary* arrived in Holsteinsborg on 1 September, with the *Bowdoin* less than twenty-four hours behind. The initial reception in this former American fishing community was proper, but far from the expected open hospitality. The crews were given permission to come ashore during the day, but were forced to return shipboard in the early evening. Once again, there was no real "liberty" for the crews, none of the famous community dances and none of the even more famous Eskimo hospitality.

According to Kennett Rawson, the *Bowdoin* weighed anchor after less than twenty-four hours and sailed about one hundred miles down the coast to Sukkertoppen, where they hoped a friendlier reception might await them. The *Peary* lingered in Holsteinsborg. Soon after the *Bowdoin* left, the Danish ship ss *Hans Egde* arrived with Inspector General Jensen aboard. Discovering the shore leave situation, Jensen immediately issued a radiogram (via the *Peary*) that gave MacMillan and his expedition "full permission to land anyplace in the southern Greenland district." Thanks to that radiogram, all hands aboard the *Bowdoin* were warmly received in Sukkertoppen.

Governor General Jensen also extended full privileges of the port of

Holsteinsborg to the *Peary*. The governor's welcome had an immediate affect on the previously reticent residents, and the *Peary* remained there for another four days. All hands had a good time.

At 4:00 A.M. on 5 August, the *Peary* left Holsteinsborg for the two-hundred-mile run to Godthab, where it would receive coal. The passage south to Godthab was nothing like the run south from Igloodahouny, as McDonald reported to the National Geographic Society in his daily report of 6 September:

> Yesterday morning Saturday Sept. 5th at four A.M. we steamed out of Holsteinsborg where we had been entertained royally by Governor Bistrup and ex-Governor Rasmussen—Barometer rising—we bucked a heavy head sea and head wind until four A.M. this morning when it became exceedingly foggy, and we should be now opposite our port, Godthab, where we are to receive our coal—Godthab lies fourteen miles up a fjord with myriads of inlands [islands] at the entrance—The entire coast of Greenland at this point is studded with islands, and it is extremely difficult to distinguish one group from the other—The only thing marking the islands outside Godthab is a small beacon unlighted standing about six feet high with a four foot globe of basket-work on its top—not easily located even in clear weather—Under full check not making more than one mile an hour, we carefully picked our way thru the fog and at all times encountered a heavy sea—The *Peary*, having practically no coal in its bunkers and being heavily laden on its upper decks with the three aeroplanes which offered great wind resistance as well as weight, listed over like a schooner under full sail in the heavy wind and sea—only three of the personnel appeared for breakfast and they negotiated their meal of coffee and toast standing up—Thru the fog we at last made a group of islands but there were breakers all around us, and we dared not proceed further—We dropped our hook and have been riding the heavy sea all day, Sunday, and as this message is dictated at midnight Sunday night we are still at anchor the fog thick the wind strong and the sea heavy—We are hoping the fog will lift as our coal, now reduced to approximately five tons, cannot hold out much longer—Our radio is shut down tonight to give the generators an opportunity to dry: they have been thoroughly drenched by a port hole being left open—We will get under way the moment the fog lifts.

Godthab

The storm abated near dawn and the *Peary* sailed up the beautiful sixty-mile-long fjord to Godthab, then as now the seat of Greenlandic government. For the first time, the men caught a glimpse of why Leif Eriksson chose the name Greenland. Throughout the remainder of his career, MacMillan made many references to this fjord:

> . . . as beautiful as it is long, revealing a composite picture of Norway and Switzerland—the fjords of the former, the snow-capped peaks of the latter. It was interesting to know that within a few yards of the shore, we were sailing in waters nearly 2,000 feet deep; that some of the peaks towered almost from the water's edge to more than 5,000 feet in height! And more interesting was it to realize that we were sailing the same waters traversed by the hardy Vikings in their high-prowed open boats more than 900 years ago![2]

The *Peary* lay at anchor in Godthab fjord for ten days for rest, recreation, and reprovisioning. The length of the stay was at least partly due to waiting some time for a Danish coastal collier to arrive in Godthab with the *Peary*'s (and Godthab's) coal supply. The days were taken up with entertainment, both formal and informal (written invitations were exchanged in some cases), between the *Peary* party and leaders of the Godthab community. The crew took additional time making the ship seaworthy for the journey south.

On 8 September, concerned about wind resistance and the need to clear deck space, McDonald requested of Byrd that "the aeroplane wings which are now lashed in a vertical position running fore and aft on the port side of the ship just abaft the beam lashed to our after port davits be laid in a horizontal position on the deck and that the heavy boarding of one side of the wing crates be either heaved over board or dismantled and moved below decks. This for the purpose of reducing wind resistance on the upper deck." On 10 September, McDonald reminded Byrd of the wing storage problems, stating in a letter:

> In order to expedite matters and cause no delay I will appreciate it if you will authorize the placing of the wings in a horizontal position on the port side today. Captain Steele and myself this morning made the measurements and

find that there is sufficient room for the wings in the location selected, and Captain Steele will be very glad to give you what assistance you may require from the crew.

The tone and the frequency of the exchanges on this and related matters indicate that Byrd and McDonald were beginning to show the stress of the trip.

After a dinner party in the home of His Excellency Governor Simony, governor of South Greenland, Commander McDonald presented him and his family with a Zenith radio, which McDonald installed himself. He then announced plans for South Greenland's first-ever radio concert to occur the next evening at the governor's residence. McDonald's report to the National Geographic Society on 10 September affords a snapshot of those days:

> Still in harbor at Godthab waiting for coal. The ship with our coal was due today but has not arrived. Fog thick and wind high, and the Danish ship has no radio. MacMillan still at Sukkertoppen weather permitting will leave at 3 A.M. for Godthab. Danish naval vessel *Island Falk* and Danish government ship *Hans Egde* having on board Minister of the Interior of Denmark, Haug and Director of Greenland Dangaard Jensen on board are lying in harbor here with us. We have this day presented to the Governor General of Southern Greenland a radio receiving set for his residence, and it is now being installed. The first radio concert in a southern Greenland home we hope to have tomorrow evening, and we can picture no place that radio would be more appreciated than here during the long winter night. Last evening on the *Peary* we were entertained by concerts from stations all over the United States including five Chicago stations.

The first radio concert in a southern Greenland home occurred the next evening and was a great success. The guests enjoyed a special broadcast from Chicago that was received, at least in part, through the courtesy of the two Danish vessels in the harbor. They had each been using their rather poor spark-gap transmitting equipment, which emitted a great deal of interference at many frequencies. The ships acquiesced to a special request from McDonald for radio silence during the scheduled broadcast from Chicago.

McDonald and members of the Naval Arctic Unit formed friendships with the crews of these two Danish ships. This was particularly true of the Danish Royal Navy vessel HMS *Island Falk*—probably because during a savage storm which penetrated the fjord late one night the *Peary* saved the ten-man crew of the *Island Falk*'s steam launch as she was sinking. The near disaster was reported in a *National Geographic* press release on 10 September:

We are lying in harbor at Godthab. A terrific gale struck tonight (September 9). The wind is ranging between seventy and eighty miles an hour and at times greater. The Danish naval vessel, *Island Faulk* [*sic*], is also in harbor with us. The harbor is well protected only on one side where the Stag Horn Mountain rises to a height of 5,700 feet. The balance is comparatively exposed.

Shortly after the gale hit us we heard the screams of men almost alongside the *Peary*. Our entire personnel rushed on deck and the sight that greeted our eyes was the small power boat of the *Island Faulk* [*sic*] full of Danish naval sailors, towing a small dory loaded with another group of sailors struggling helplessly against the terrific sea. The wind and seas crashed them against the side of the *Peary*. One Danish sailor, Laurits Christensen, had forethought enough to throw the heavy tow line off the power boat, which we made fast as it swamped and immediately sank. The dory swamped immediately afterwards.

The Danish sailors were helpless in this frigid Greenland water with temperature approximately 20 degrees, and the sea a seething mass of foam. All were clinging to the sides of the sunken boats made fast to the *Peary*. Never have I seen a greater display of unselfishness, consideration for the other man and calmness in an emergency.

The water was sweeping [over] the many hands on the deck of the *Peary*, ready to pull them aboard. But our rail is six feet above the water line. The Danes seemed to a man to realize that they one by one must be taken aboard up the line. There was no fighting, no man trying to push ahead of the other. One by one we hauled them aboard, recovering every man of the two boats.

The *Island Faulk* [*sic*] was signaled by flags. We advised them that all their men were on board the *Peary*. The men slipped [off] their wet clothes and dressed in dry clothes of the personnel of the *Peary*. As this message is dictated they are all sleeping comfortable in our dining salon . . .

The sunken boats broke the line a moment after we had hauled the men aboard. As this message is dictated the gale is still raging and although we have out our anchors, of which we have two holding, we have steam up ready to put our nose into it if the anchors let go. The Norwegian trawler, *Iris,* which also is lying in the harbor, broke her mooring and went ashore. Her crew abandoned her without loss of life.

We are thankful to be in harbor tonight . . .[3]

That savage storm was the first of several that would plague and endanger the ships and men throughout the remainder of the expedition.

On 14 September, the *Bowdoin* arrived in Godthab having been delayed both by the hospitality in Sukkertoppen and by a major storm further up the coast. The *Peary* was now fully provisioned, had full bunkers, and was ready to sail for home. MacMillan wished to remain in Godthab and sail some forty-five miles farther inland to the head of the fjord to inspect the nine-hundred-year-old ruins of a small Norse village and a church located there. The scientific party aboard the *Peary* was transferred to the *Bowdoin* for that purpose. MacMillan later reported that the ruins were well preserved and had filled him with a feeling of reverence. The *Peary* sailed at 3:00 P.M. on 16 September 1925, making directly for Battle Harbor, Labrador.

More Dangerous Crossings

By mid-September, what was to be an active hurricane season was well under way, and the remnants of several storms were to plague the expedition as it fought its way west and south toward home. Crossing Davis Strait to Labrador at this season in any year is dangerous. In 1925, it was especially perilous. Today, it is hard for us to visualize sea travel like this: suffering raging gales and freezing seawater, all the while dodging icebergs with a badly overloaded ship. It was a very dangerous crossing in extremely dangerous waters. During the same season in the previous year, a number of major vessels, crewed by experienced northern seamen, were lost to storms in these same waters. More ships were lost during the fall of 1925 as well. As on the trip north, both the *Peary* and the *Bowdoin* were sailing directly into harm's way as they returned south.

The *Peary* cleared the Greenland coast by late afternoon and was immediately struck by "fresh" winds that soon became a full gale. The accompanying radio operator's typescript of McDonald's report to the National Geographic Society on 19 September actually understates the danger due to the *Peary*'s heavy deck load. The added wind resistance of the airplanes secured in their cradles high above the waterline on the aft deck also affected the ship's ability to make the crossing safely. The *Peary* made landfall on the Labrador coast near the small community of Bateau and immediately sought shelter from the seventy-five-mile-per-hour gale in a nearby cove. The *Peary* had completed the six-hundred-mile crossing in less than three days. The next day, as McDonald reported, the *Peary* moved to Battle Harbor:

> At three P.M. September 16th, *Peary* sailed from Godthab—Cleared the Greenland reefs by five P.M. then blowing fresh from the north—We have made a record run and were exactly on our course picking up South Wolf Island 53-42 North Latitude about noon today.—We have had a gale most of the way across.—Our radio antenna was torn into bits by the gale—Repaired this morning blown out again this afternoon and now in operation again.— We came around Roundhill Island in a seventy-five mile gale cleared the reefs and are now snugly anchored in harbor of Sandy Bay on the Island of Ponds just outside Bateau Harbor 53-24 North Latitude—55-48 West Longitude. Great credit is due Captain Steele for his excellent navigation and handling of the ship in the gale, and the *Peary* with its heavy deck load has proven itself to be a wonderful sea boat—Many times however we have been thankful that we covered the portholes with steel plates. During the last day few have appeared for meals, and those who did have been forced to eat standing up—Our cargo is all safe, we lost nothing overboard.—Weather permitting we will run to Battle Harbor tomorrow.—MacMillan is still in harbor at Godthab waiting for favorable weather.—We too are watching our weather closely as the equinox is only a little more than twenty four hours away.—And we are all glad to be in harbor tonight as the wind is howling at such a rate that even the fishermen in the little village we are anchored off from have been unable to come out to visit us.

During this crossing, MacMillan and McDonald decided to hold the *Peary* at Battle Harbor until the *Bowdoin* was across and then move the *Peary* south to Curling, halfway down the Newfoundland coast, again to await the arrival of the slower *Bowdoin*. The reasons for this decision are not recorded in surviving accounts, but probably relate to using one ship to rescue the other, if necessary. It is clear from MacMillan's diary that he was very pleased to have, for the first time, the ship-to-ship shortwave radio aboard the vessels.

The *Peary* lay in Battle Harbor for the next four days, awaiting the *Bowdoin*'s crossing. It is evident that McDonald spent much of his time in business activities, exchanging numerous radiograms with Zenith head-quarters in Chicago. One of the first asked S. I. Marks, then a Zenith executive, to make sure that Sport Herrmann had the $20,000 to $30,000 capital nec-essary to fund the upcoming Chicago Radio Show. If he did not, McDonald's mother was to go to the First National Bank, sign for herself and McDonald, and borrow the money. A follow-up telegram to Marks read, "Radio me what took place at New York show—who had the sensational models?"

There were several exchanges with the National Geographic Society dur-ing the four days spent at anchor in Battle Harbor. A number of transmis-sions were intended to clarify the erroneous claims of a New Zealand radio amateur who claimed to hold a world distance record, having heard the *Peary*'s transmissions from Etah. The confusion was almost certainly caused by the failure of *Bowdoin*'s radio operator, Reinartz, to transmit some of the official messages from the expedition to the society.

Lost with All Hands?

Gales continued to rage outside Battle Harbor most of the time. Due to the curtailing of the flight schedule at Etah, the *Peary* was still carrying thirty-nine barrels of aviation gasoline. McDonald reluctantly made the decision to offload the aviation gasoline (with full documentation for Navy Secretary Wilbur) to lighten the ship and improve her balance "in a blow." McDon-ald's 22 September report to the National Geographic Society indicated how dangerous the journey had been:

> Still in Battle Harbor, Gale outside in straits we are glad to be in. It now develops that all the natives of Battle Harbor were surprised to see us return as it was agreed to a man among the fishermen of this settlement that when

we left they would never see the *Peary* again, the *Peary* would never return. They did not believe she was an icebreaker, and when I told them the *Peary* broke the ice for the *Bowdoin* going thru Melville Bay they gazed at me and were too polite to make comments, and I know that none of them believed me.

Battle Harbor authorities informed McDonald that the coastal passenger and freight steamship, the ss *Home,* was missing and feared lost in the gales. The ship usually made a weekly round trip between Curling, Newfoundland, and Battle Harbor, calling at most ports along the coast. She had left Curling several days previous, was overdue at Battle Harbor, and had not been seen at any of her normal stops. The *Home*'s sister ship, the ss *Ethie,* had been lost with all hands on a similar run five years before. McDonald immediately volunteered to use the *Peary* as a search and rescue vessel if the *Home* was not located within forty-eight hours. McDonald also offered the services of the expedition's one operable airplane and clashed briefly with Byrd when he opposed this use of the plane. Fortunately for all, the *Home* was found before the *Peary* set out; the storm was so bad that she had to travel far north of Battle Harbor (her northern terminus) before she found a safe harbor to wait out the blow.

As the days passed at Battle Harbor, McDonald became increasingly concerned about the fate of the *Bowdoin,* which had left Godthab on the morning of 21 September. For over forty-eight hours after the ship had been under way, and for reasons he never explained, radio operator Reinartz ceased keeping the thrice-daily radio schedule between the *Bowdoin* and the *Peary.* McDonald and the *Peary* radio operators were not unduly worried when Reinartz missed the first scheduled contact, thinking that the *Bowdoin*'s wire radio antenna may have parted in the storm as the *Peary*'s had twice during the crossing. However, as the ominous silence stretched beyond twenty-four hours, McDonald had to assume that the *Bowdoin* was lost. *Peary* radio operators McGee and Gray began calling the *Bowdoin* on an hourly basis. A day later, with still no response to the *Peary*'s hourly radio calls, the ship was preparing to sail out into the storm to search for the *Bowdoin* when Reinartz casually radioed that the *Bowdoin* was across and safe. She was far to the north in Jack Lane's Bay. When told that MacMillan was in, McDonald radioed his concern to his friend:

You have certainly had us worried as we have not heard a sound from you from 5:30 P.M. on Monday night until 5:30 P.M. on Thursday night. Last night we asked the amateurs in the United States if they had heard you, and they said they had not heard a peep. I was particularly worried because it has been wonderful radio weather. We have had wonderful results clearing several thousand words in an afternoon. We work the states almost at will; time seems to mean nothing. When the amateurs told us last not [night] they had not heard you, we started calling you once every hour during the last twenty-four.

Reinartz merely said tonight that you expect to be in Jack Lanes Bay tomorrow and that he could not copy us but even that was good news. I assume that you have had a very rough passage and probably Reinartz [was] seasick. Frankly Mac, I was so worried for your safety that I was prepared if I did not hear from you on Friday to leave the entire Navy personnel at the hospital at Battle Harbor, load the three aeroplanes on the dock, take all the coal they had in Battle Harbor and go back north in search for you. I said nothing about it to anyone except Captain Steele and Dr. Davidoff. I told the doctor of my intentions as he was considering staying on with us in hopes we could beat the ss *Home* to Curling. Davidoff has promised me that on his return to the states he will positively make no newspaper statement of any kind except to *National Geographic.* I did not tell even the natives or any of the rest of our personnel about any of my worries except the radio operator Brazill who could hear us calling you once every hour and knew that we were not in communication.

This critical three-day gap in communication was apparently the "last straw" as far as Reinartz was concerned. McDonald thought about the situation for over a week and then radioed MacMillan that he was leaving the *Peary*'s second radio operator, Gray, at Sydney to await the arrival of the *Bowdoin* two days later. Gray was to replace Reinartz as the *Bowdoin*'s radio operator for the remainder of the dangerous journey home.

The *Bowdoin*'s passage across to Labrador had been a very rough, fast trip, and she too was terribly overloaded with a deck load of aviation gasoline. MacMillan saw the mountains of Cape Mugford through driving mist on the morning of 24 September, and the *Bowdoin* struggled all day against gale-force winds and heavy seas to make landfall. They were unsuccessful and turned southwest to run straight for Windy Tickle and Jack Lane's Bay. There, they were greeted joyfully the next morning at the Bromfield homestead; given the weather and the lateness of the season, the Bromfields had assumed that the expedition had either been frozen in by the northern ice pack or lost with all hands.

MacMillan and McDonald wished to have both ships available to support each other; they also wanted to return simultaneously to Wiscasset. For these reasons, they decided to have the much faster *Peary* lay over in several ports along the coast; she would meet the *Bowdoin* near Monhegan Island, Maine, for the official return to American shores. Physician Davidoff made arrangements to leave the expedition and join the ss *Home* so that he could return to Boston in time to take his new appointment at Boston's Peter Bent Brigham Hospital. On Davidoff's strong recommendation, Lieutenant Commander Byrd sent Chief Boatswain Earl Reber with him. (Reber was suffering his third serious stomach ulcer attack since he had been released from the Philadelphia Navy hospital in mid-April to join the expedition.)

Hopscotching Down the Coast Toward Home

With MacMillan and the *Bowdoin* safe in Jack Lane's Bay to the north, the *Peary* set off south to Curling, Newfoundland, to await the *Bowdoin* in more comfortable circumstances. Curling was located on a beautiful deep bay; more important to the weary crew, it was large enough to have an inn. All *Peary* hands had now lived aboard in crowded conditions for over ninety days.

Unfortunately, the weather deteriorated even further as they moved down the coast. After only a few hours steaming, they were again forced to seek shelter in the bay behind Point Amour after being driven there by an easterly gale. For the second time during their voyage they lay near the eerie wreck of the HMS *Raleigh*, a reminder, if they needed one, of their own predicament. With the weather still very poor, they left Point Amour the next morning then crossed the Strait of Belle Isle to the Newfoundland coast through what proved to be one of the most violent gales ever experienced there. McDonald related the experience to a reporter in Halifax several days later and recalled that at times the *Peary* was almost completely submerged. The huge waves actually shattered some of the portholes in the main cabin, flooding the cabins and causing damage above and below decks. The wings of the three Loenings, wrapped in tarpaulins and secured on the main deck, were broken and twisted from the force of the elements. Without the long experience and seamanship of the *Peary*'s captain, George Steele, the *Peary* would likely have been lost with all hands. A rumrunner making for Sydney through the strait that same night foundered, and a number of lives were lost.

They made it across to Bonne Bay and their destination of Curling, Newfoundland, but just barely. There was enough serious damage in the engine room that the *Peary* would have to stop in Halifax after a few days of rest in Curling.

McDonald's 26 September report to the National Geographic Society described in detail the difficult crossing:

Left Forteau Bay inside Point Amour daylight and averaged better than ten miles an hour to Bonne Bay where we are thankful to be lying quiet tonight. Had gale and heavy sea all day, and *Peary* never had more water on her decks than she had today. Our port rail was completely under many times caused principally by the heavy hurricane deck load of airplanes and our light load of coal in our bunkers. Aeroplane wings on main deck on port side all damaged. Weather permitting we will sail at daylight. *Bowdoin* reports leaving Hopedale in morning for Battle Harbor.

Hostility between McDonald and Byrd

Tempers flared between McDonald and Byrd on 26–27 September over the lashing down of the navy material. A 26 September letter to Byrd from McDonald stated:

After our experience this day however I again repeat my request that you properly make fast the Navy material, this being a reiteration of my request of five P.M. this afternoon when I told you that within one hour we would be in the lee and would leave at daylight weather permitting. We have been here in port since 5:30 P.M., yet no move has been made to make fast Navy equipment. I repeat that our intention is to leave at daylight, and the Navy equipment should be made fast as it should have been when we left Etah.

Upon receiving the letter ("about ten twenty o'clock [P.M.]") Byrd went to check and indicated that Rocheville, Bennett, Nold, and Francis had put extra lashings on the wings. According to a letter written by Byrd on 27 September and signed by all members of the Naval Unit:

> A little later McDonald appeared on the port side of the ship outside my stateroom apparently in an excited state of mind and asked me to come out and look at the lashings on the Navy equipment on the gangway on the main deck. After some unintelligible remarks about the lashings put by Captain Steele on the wings on the port side, we went to the starboard side to look over the wings and lines there. Everything in McDonald's manner indicated that he doubted that any work had been done on the lashings since reaching port. In other words he doubted that I had told the truth. He requested that I send for the officers and men of the Naval Unit. While they were dressing, he threatened me with a court of inquiry using profane and uncontrolled language. The lines around the wings showed some slight slack due to a thorough and continual wetting and drying they had in the seaway, and McDonald called attention to this and stated in the presence of several witnesses that it was criminal negligence ... a reflection on the Naval Unit and very humiliating to me in that it was made before officials of the ship ... When the members of the Naval Unit arrived, McDonald procured as stenographer, Mr. Gray, and proceeded to question the petty officers. It was soon disclosed that my statements to McDonald had been correct . . . When McDonald's "would-be board of investigation" repaired to the mess room the heat of the room soon disclosed the fact that McDonald apparently was intoxicated . . . In a few minutes McDonald returned to the mess room and in the presence of the Naval Unit stated that he did not like me . . . I am putting this in writing because I know that McDonald is after me, and I believe that he would not hesitate to do the whole Navy injury to gain his ends . . .[4]

McDonald's response to Byrd's visit was indicated in a letter the morning of 27 September:

Rocheville, Bennett and Nold spent one hour this morning from 7:30 A.M. to 8:30 A.M. making fast the navy equipment. I assume that this was following your orders, and I want you to know that I appreciate you having issued them . . .

McDonald also radioed MacMillan:

. . . We really had a tough time yesterday, and a couple times when the *Peary* went over it looked as tho she would never come back. All aeroplanes [wings] on main deck port side are ruined principally because of improper and inefficient lashing.

As they waited for the *Bowdoin*, the *Peary* party spent a full week of rest and relaxation in the comparative luxury of the most northerly inn on their route, the Glynn Mill Inn in Corner Brook, a suburb of Curling, Newfoundland. It was at the Glynn Mill Inn that a somewhat serious incident occurred between McDonald, a stickler for naval regulations, and Byrd. The incident further indicates the growing hostility between the two men. On 1 October 1925, McDonald sent the following letter to Byrd:

My dear Commander,
Last evening I was very glad to observe the removal from the register, at the Glynn Mill Inn, Corner Brook, the title "Vice Admiral USN" which you originally placed on the register.

It was extremely embarrassing to me when even Americans asked to be introduced to the Admiral, to be forced to tell them there was no Admiral on board the *Peary*.

If in the future while on this expedition you again have occasion to register at any hotel in the ports we may land, I will appreciate it if you will place after your name your proper rank.

Byrd responded on 2 October:

My dear Commander,
I have your letter requesting that if I have occasion to register at any hotel in future that I place the proper rank after my name.

I wish to tell you that I never put any rank after my name when I register.

That of course, includes the occasion in question. I always simply put "USN" after my name. I registered at the Glynn Mill Inn at the request of the clerk for a meal which I took. If there are any exceptions to this rule, I do not remember them.

The night of the dance when I discovered that someone had put "Vice Admiral" before my name (undoubtedly as a joke) I called the attention of Bennett and Sorensen to the fact that the "Vice Admiral" was not in my writing and immediately scratched it out.

Also on 2 October, Bennett and Sorensen filed a signed affidavit on Byrd's behalf supporting Byrd's account of the incident. They added: "We consider this just another indecent move on McDonald's part to get some technicality on Commander Byrd. It seems evident to everyone that McDonald has been trying hard to trump up something against [him]."

McDonald responded to Byrd on 3 October 1925:

My Dear Commander,
Acknowledging your good letter of October second. I may be mistaken in the handwriting, and I sincerely trust that I am, and I sincerely trust that the statement of the acting manager and the photograph of the register are in error.

Despite that incident, it is apparent from other correspondence that all hands had a very good time at the inn in Curling. In a letter of appreciation to the innkeeper, McDonald spoke of "our delight in having the pleasure of meeting such a delightful group of people as we found at the Glynn Mill Inn. To us it was a breath of heaven." McDonald went on to promise a special broadcast from WJAZ in November to all of their "friends around the Bay of Islands."

Further Dangerous Crossings

On 2 October, the *Peary* party had an uneventful voyage to Sydney, Nova Scotia, and paused there for two more days before moving south to the great harbor at Halifax. MacMillan and the *Bowdoin* were still lagging behind and proceeded south down the Labrador coast as quickly as possible. MacMillan, writing in the November 1925 *National Geographic*, recorded the *Bowdoin*'s run in his usual understated manner:

> No time to be lost. We were under way at daybreak, bound south for the Moravian settlement at Hopedale. Here we rid ourselves of that frightful load of Navy gasoline. The *Bowdoin* was now a different ship. Her deck was clear. She was stripped for action. Driving before rain and wind, the ship swept down the Labrador coast a frightened bird. Off Cape Strawberry our main gaff snapped, but a new one, ordered by radio, awaited us at Battle Harbor. Only one night here to fit our new stick and lace on the sail and we were away, heading down through the Belleisle [*sic*] Strait for home.

The *Bowdoin* arrived in North Sydney and Sydney proper on the morning of 6 October, two days after the *Peary* left to move south to Halifax. There was an impromptu, but nonetheless warm, welcome; throngs of well-wishers gathered at the dock. The *Bowdoin* paused for only half a day to take on fuel oil and provisions; all hands made for the local barbershop to prepare themselves for the welcome that awaited them five hundred miles to the southwest.

After the harrowing experiences encountered so far, and so close to home, all aboard must have felt that surely the worst was behind them. It was not. MacMillan's account, again chronicled in the November 1925 *National Geographic:*

> If wind and sea had remained from the same quarter, we would have had a comfortable night, but as darkness came on the wind whipped around from the southeast to northwest, with vivid flashes of lightning and driving rain. A nasty cross-sea caught the *Bowdoin* from every direction. She shipped tons of water over her bow and over both rails, threatening to wash some of my men overboard.
>
> We finally shortened down to a foresail alone, to ease ship a bit. In taking down our forestaysail, or jumbo, Salmon was almost completely buried by a sea which swept over the bow, and Melkon was taken off his feet. Working in the pitch dark, they did well to remain on deck.
>
> Fearing for their safety and not hearing a sound above the roar of the wind and rush of waters, I left the wheel for a moment and ran forward to

learn if they were still there. I found them tugging on the sail, endeavoring to lash it down to the boom. I had no sooner reached the wheel than the third member of my watch, Rawson, our fifteen-year-old [sic] cabin boy, was knocked down by a sea which swept aft along the deck, flush with the low rail—a close call.

At this moment the ominous slatting and banging of a sail revealed that the lacing on our foregaff had given way. This meant the loss of our most valued sail unless it could be taken in at once. "All hands on deck!" and up they came with a rush, showing that each man had tumbled into his bunk "all standing," as we say at sea.

No man on shore can properly visualize such a scene—roar of wind, swash of water, snap and crack of canvas and ropes—a little ship buried in froth; dark oilskin-clad forms working rapidly here and there; the blackness, punctuated with order from the officer in charge, as wave after wave reached over the rail, ending with a thud against lifeboat or cabin.

With engine full speed ahead, we were dropping backward, and there were times when the *Bowdoin* seemed to have decided to go back North. She headed east and fairly ran away with the bit in her teeth and her jaws frothing.

But the next morning was glorious—a beautiful fall day, and good weather. All day we raced along in under the land—a glorious sail—with the *Peary*, which had been awaiting us at Halifax, slowly creeping up. Not until we rounded Cape Sable, however, and were well in toward Seal Island, on the last leg of our voyage, did she forge past us, her lighted cabins giving her the appearance of an ocean liner. Three long blasts of her whistle ended the race, as she crept ahead and disappeared into the night, heading up for Monhegan Island, off the Maine coast, nearly abreast of Wiscasset.

Monhegan Island

All the next day, the two ships headed southwest for home. The *Peary* arrived at Monhegan Island, anchored in the inner harbor about midday on 9 October, and was greeted by a crowd of over fifty people who had taken the passenger ferry *Novelty* out from Wiscasset to greet the expedition. Included in the crowd were news reporters and family members of many aboard both expedition vessels. The next day, the *Boston Post* headline touted the return of the expedition with banner headlines: "VOYAGE INTO ARCTIC GREAT SUCCESS, DECLARES EXPLORER MACMILLAN." Late that afternoon, the *Peary* entertained the ladies with a dinner in the wardroom. According to Mrs. M. A. Schur, the food was of poor quality and quantity. Apparently, the expedition was just about out of supplies. Seeing the meager offering and sensing the distress of the visitors, Lieutenant Commander Byrd returned to his cabin and soon reappeared with an armload of food. After a brief awkward period, Mrs. Schur related, all of the men, including Byrd, left the wardroom. Later, everyone except Byrd returned.

By 4:00 P.M. that same afternoon, the *Bowdoin* sighted Matinicus Rocks, the most northeasterly point of American and Maine soil. Just at dusk and on schedule, the *Bowdoin* dropped anchor in Dead Man's Cove on Monhegan Island. The island was MacMillan's favorite staging port and lay some twenty miles off the coast of Maine. The *Bowdoin* dropped her hook in the lee of a large ledge in the outer harbor to await the morning; her crew had arrived "home" just in time to sail at dawn and reach Wiscasset for their scheduled welcome by Governor Brewster and the citizens of Maine. Mother Nature had other plans.

At 5:00 A.M., the *Bowdoin* crew was awakened by the all-too-familiar slatting of the halyards and the roar of the wind through the rigging. They were in the opening act of what would long be remembered on the New England coast as the "Great Gale of October Tenth." Their anchorage was fairly protected by the ledge but was open to the westerly swell that built all morning. By midafternoon, the *Bowdoin* was surrounded by a maelstrom that MacMillan described later as a "chaos of white water." The anchor chain stood out like an iron bar and the stern was within a few feet of the rocks. If the anchor slipped, the *Bowdoin* would have instantly been on the rocks and destroyed. MacMillan finally decided that he had no choice; the anchor was slowly winched in and the gallant *Bowdoin* fought her way foot by foot directly to the windward into the teeth of the hurricane. When, at last, she had made enough way, the helm was put smartly over and she ran before the storm into the inner harbor to join the *Peary*.

The expedition and its guests rather gratefully waited out the storm the

McDonald, Schur, Floyd Bennett, and Byrd pose here at the dock in Wiscasset upon their return in October 1925. When the authors first discovered this photograph, they misidentified it as having been taken on the way north. The canvas-wrapped wings on the deck of the *Peary*, immediately behind the four, prove that the photo was taken upon their return. Their decidedly disgruntled expressions in this photo are now much more understandable.
Schur Family Papers

remainder of that Saturday and all day Sunday. By Sunday evening it was obvious that the blow was at an end, and plans were made to leave Monhegan at dawn. Fourteen-year-old Kennett Rawson wrote in his book, *A Boy's Eye View of the Arctic:*

> As it would still be rough, the ladies who had joined us at Battle Harbor [*sic*] were requested to go up to Wiscasset on the *Peary* that they might be spared the discomforts of a trip on the smaller vessel.[5]

Monday morning arrived and the *Peary* gave a long toot on her siren and pulled out from the dock. She passed quite close to us, and we observed that her decks were nearly deserted. Where were the ladies? In a few moments we knew. Boat after boat appeared, loaded to the gunwales with their numbers. Not more than a handful had gone on the *Peary;* contrary to all instructions they had refused to go on our consort, and insisted on going on the *Bowdoin* ... A good many of them were soon seasick, but in a short time we had come into the quiet waters on Boothbay Harbor. Up the green bordered channels we picked our way, our decks crowded with cheering visitors. Slowly we reeled off the miles until at last we entered the Sheepscot, then with flags flying we proceeded up the river, and at last amidst the roar of steam whistles and the cheers of the multitude assembled on the shore, the Commander uttered those long awaited words: "Let go."

The delayed welcome in "little Wiscasset" was at least as tumultuous as the departure ceremonies had been. Governor Brewster of Maine and Adm. D. E. Dismukes, commandant of the Kittery Navy Yard, led the ceremonies. Col. John C. Wright, commander of the Portland harbor defenses, represented the army; the entire congressional delegation of the state of Maine was in attendance, as were the president of the Maine state senate and the speaker of Maine's House of Representatives. Contemporary accounts record heavy attendance by Bowdoin College students and the citizenry of Maine. Kennett Rawson described the day's end:

Soon the visitors had departed, and we were left alone on our sturdy little ship. We had sailed six thousand miles, crossed the Arctic Circle twice, fought through the dread reaches of Melville Bay, launched our planes over the unknown Arctic, and returned all unscathed. Now all was ended: "Timakeza," as the Eskimo would say.

SIX

The Importance of the
MacMillan Expedition

*I*N THIS MODERN ERA OF ROUTINE TRANSPOLAR FLIGHTS by jet airliners carrying hundreds of relaxed, confident, shirtsleeved passengers, it is difficult for us to visualize the conspicuous bravery with which the men of the 1925 MacMillan Arctic Expedition faced extreme danger. It is hard to appreciate the level of determination and grit with which they endured and produced in conditions of almost continual physical and mental hardship. All members of this expedition, aviators and sailors alike, gambled their lives on many occasions. They wagered on themselves—their own abilities and character—and on their comrades. The modesty with which the expedition members recorded their experiences is impressive. The men's journals also are marked by instance after instance when they paused to record the awesome beauty of the sea, the ice, and the rugged northern landscape.

The MacMillan Arctic Expedition of 1925 has actually *gained* in historical importance over time. It marked the first significant use of radio communication by a polar expedition, significantly influenced the history of long-distance communication, and marked the first reasonably successful use of aviation for polar exploration. No one realized it at the time, of course, but this expedition also marked the "changing of the guard" of polar exploration. Although Donald B. MacMillan would make dozens more trips to the Far North and would fill in many blank spots on northern maps, this expedition was his last in the national spotlight as an explorer involved with high technology "firsts." More important, though, this particular MacMillan expedition marked the handoff from the seaborne, sledge-based, terribly isolated expeditions of Nansen, Greely, Peary, Scott, and Shackleton to the airborne, machine-driven, communications-linked worlds of Byrd, Lindbergh, and eventually Neil Armstrong.

At the press conference upon his return to Chicago, Commander McDonald was perhaps speaking for the entire expedition when he said, "The Arctic explorer's life ain't what it used to be" now that aviation and radio had arrived in the Arctic.

Radio

The science and technology of radio matured significantly in the years between the 1923 and 1925 MacMillan expeditions. Nevertheless, true "shortwave" radio was in its infancy. Even in the amateur ranks, very few operators had shortwave capabilities in the summer of 1925. The Zenith-funded efforts of John Reinartz, R. H. G. Mathews, and Karl Hassel to popularize the shortwave spectrum among amateurs via this expedition have gone largely unrecognized. Circuitry for both receiving and transmitting shortwave signals was made available gratis by Zenith to the amateur community before and after the expedition. The opportunities thus provided to radio amateurs all over the world to "work" such exotic locations as the various ports of call visited by the *Bowdoin* and the *Peary* must have been a significant stimulus to the migration of amateurs to the shortwave spectrum.

The ability of powerful shortwave equipment, like that aboard the two MacMillan ships, to communicate almost at will over planetary distances, day or night, was a real breakthrough in the history of both exploration and communications. Even if the expedition had turned back after the coaling incident at Godhavn, Greenland, the fact that McDonald and Byrd could easily communicate with MacMillan, then almost one thousand miles away in Hopedale, Labrador, and with the navy and the National Geographic Society, twenty-three hundred miles to the south, both day and night, would have revolutionized polar exploration. The fact that both ships communicated with the U.S. Fleet, then in New Zealand, and with radio amateurs in southern Australia played a significant role in the navy's decision to adopt shortwave radio for fleet communications.

MacMillan's 1925 expedition diary entries, however, largely focus on the ability of the new equipment to provide instantaneous voice communications between the two ships. Freed from telegraphic code and specialist radio operators, the ability of one ship's captain to talk to the other, directly and at will, proved to be immensely useful in heavy weather and, especially, in the ice fields. McDonald himself was particularly impressed with the potential of using shortwave transmissions to conduct business and commerce over long distances. He was in daily contact with either S. I. Marks, then general manager of Zenith, or H. H. Roemer, director of sales promotion. Upon the explorer's arrival in Chicago, a reporter remarked to McDonald, "You are probably very anxious to get to your office to see how your business has been doing in your absence." McDonald answered:

> What do you mean by "my absence?" I have been in constant communication with the Zenith offices by our short wave apparatus. In fact, I believe that I was in closer touch than when I am actually in the office. That is true, at least when one considers the thousands and thousands of words which passed between us each week.

The entertainment aspects of radio—programs from the United States, daily news broadcasts from the U.S. and Europe, broadcasts of Eskimo singing to the U.S. and elsewhere, and radio concerts for local residents in northern ports—played an important role in this expedition. Most of these aspects of radio, however, had become almost routine in the two years between the two radio-equipped MacMillan Arctic expeditions—so routine, in fact, that they were almost totally ignored in the logs of all three radio operators.

The 1925 MacMillan Arctic Expedition's role in influencing the history of navy communications and, through the navy, the overall history of long-distance communications, was lost for a complex set of reasons, which are addressed in the afterword. However, the expedition and Zenith's "very significant role in the introduction and early history of short-wave radio in the Navy," and thus in the history of long-distance communications, was finally officially acknowledged by the navy in a Navy Department letter to McDonald dated 21 October 1946.

Aviation

In the most pragmatic terms, the flight operations of this expedition have to be considered, at best, a partial success. Two caches of supplies were laid down for future operations, but neither was even halfway to Cape Thomas Hubbard, the intended forward operating base on Axel Heiberg Island. This must have been a bitter pill for Lieutenant Commander MacMillan, who had used Cape Hubbard as his jumping-off place in 1914 for his sledge trip far out over the Polar Sea. Further, the unexpected vagaries of wind- and tide-borne ice opening and closing potential landing areas near cache sites had proven that the entire concept of short flights leapfrogging toward the Pole from cache to cache was flawed. Air navigation techniques and instruments also proved to be totally inadequate in the difficult polar environment. Most of all, the aviators had failed to explore any part of the huge Polar Sea area, which might have contained a significant and very strategic landmass.

The winter of 1924–25 was the coldest in living memory, and thus many areas of normally open water were ice-bound. That fact alone would likely have made the main aviation mission of long-range exploration impossible. The day-to-day weather at Etah also proved to be much worse than even MacMillan expected. Given less than eight total days of flying, half of those under very marginal conditions, long-range exploration was simply impossible with the technology and instrumentation available.

However, the Naval Arctic Unit, operating under *extremely* hazardous conditions, without adequate support and with aircraft which proved to be inherently unsuited to the task, managed to build a solid foundation of aeronautical experience in the Far North. Using three planes of a totally new type, these conspicuously brave aviators flew more than six thousand miles, five thousand of which were flights from Etah on work central to the mission of the expedition. From the air, they had viewed more than thirty thousand square miles of terrain, a large part of which was inaccessible to foot travel and, thus, never before seen by humans.

The flyers also gathered invaluable field experience with the Loening airframe and the newly developed inverted Liberty engine, each of which was in its first operational use on this expedition. The inversion of the Liberty engine had obviously caused problems with lubrication, especially of the rod and crankshaft bearings. These problems, which were still unresolved at the end of the expedition, appear to have been the root cause of the three failed engines which were replaced under hazardous conditions in the Far North. The lessons gained by the expedition were, apparently, rather quickly applied to all other Loening Amphibians. The plane and its inverted Liberty engine were soon performing beautifully under difficult conditions in other places. The navy used Loenings for several long surveys of the Alaskan coast, and the U.S. Marines put them to use on the Yangtze in China and elsewhere. Probably the most celebrated use of the Loenings was in the U.S. Army Pan-American Good-Will Flight. Four planes circumnavigated Central and South America, touching down in twenty-two countries in a little over four months in 1926–27.

Byrd, soon to be world renowned as a polar explorer, applied the lessons of the MacMillan expedition almost immediately and became recognized as the first person to fly over the North Pole less than a year later. Three years after that success, Byrd became the first person to fly over the South Pole. The foundations laid by the Naval Arctic Unit aviators continued to pay large dividends in World War II and in Operation Deep Freeze on the Greenland Ice Cap some thirty years after the expedition.

Afterword

$\mathscr{A}$S WE WERE PIECING TOGETHER AN ALMOST COM-
plete file of original documents of the expedition, both public and private,
we became aware that we had access to far more information about the
expedition, its participants, and their motives and behavior than did any of
the people themselves, at that time or later. During our long involvement
with this story, we developed insights that explained the historical omission
of both Zenith and Commander McDonald's crucial contributions to this
expedition as well as their impact on the development of long-distance
communications. We also became aware of the largely unacknowledged
benefits of this expedition to Richard E. Byrd's development as a leading
polar explorer. We feel it appropriate to record our insights into both of
these matters, but wish to do so outside the main text.

As the details of the expedition began to emerge from our work, we also
became very aware that the public personas and reputations of some of the
participants would be changed if this story were fully told. We briefly considered simply ignoring some of the bickering late in the journey, and even

some of the more blatant misbehavior of some participants. After some thought, we decided that we should tell the truth as we found it. Neither our readers nor the expedition participants deserve less.

We realize, too, that none of the individuals involved are available today to defend themselves, or even to explain their motives and behavior from their own points of view. From a lifetime of reading accounts of geographic expeditions, we know that many of these affairs became pressure cookers of human emotions and behavior. These experiences, usually in very crowded quarters, often on short or unhealthy rations, and almost always involving the stress of isolation and danger, tend to bring out both the best and the worst of human behavior. So it was with the 1925 MacMillan Arctic Expedition. Although we are not qualified as final arbiters of behavior, we cannot close this account without a few additional comments.

MacMillan

Donald B. MacMillan's reputation as a pillar of probity and as a leader of men under difficult circumstances survives untarnished in these pages. Nowhere in the record does he appear to have deviated from the personal reputation for understatement, honesty, and steadfast leadership that General Greely commented on in his introduction to MacMillan's account of his 1913–17 Crocker Land Expedition. Toward the end of his life, MacMillan was most proud of never having lost a man to starvation, the sea, or the cold. His long career and high standards of scholarship and leadership were an inspiration to several generations of young men. We hope that this account will encourage renewed interest in this great polar explorer.

McDonald

Eugene F. McDonald Jr.'s role in this expedition was much more extensive than he wished to be publicly known. Despite our research into his career and life for our book, *Zenith Radio: The Early Years, 1919–1935* (Atglen, Pa., 1997), we did not even suspect the scale of his leadership in the planning, the financing, and the political negotiations that made this expedition possible. As we pieced the story together, we continued to be amazed at the effectiveness and genius of this almost unknown player on the national stage.

McDonald was very upset during the expedition and remained mystified afterwards as to why he was essentially "written out" of the official navy accounts of the expedition, as well as the National Geographic Society's official press releases. In retrospect, it appears that the navy radio hierarchy was not pleased to have McDonald or Zenith receive any publicity from the expedition. In fact, the navy issued a press release during the expedition that took full credit for many of the radio "firsts" of the expedition and that all but eliminated the important role of McDonald and Zenith. Possibly, the navy radio personnel, especially in Washington, D.C., were not happy that "outsiders" from Chicago were attempting to influence navy policies related to radio communications.

Much the same distortion of the facts occurred in press releases from the National Geographic Society during August 1925, when the expedition was making daily headline news. Many of the messages sent from the *Peary* to the National Geographic Society—and, in fact, virtually all of the official daily reports of the expedition—were written and signed by McDonald, yet in the society's press releases, they were invariably attributed to Donald B. MacMillan, even if it was impossible for him to have written them. McDonald sent radiograms to E. F. Roemer at Zenith asking him to find out why this was happening. Possibly, the society was somewhat reluctant to have its expedition's cosponsor prominently featured in the press releases. Possibly, the confusion and upset in communications caused by John Reinartz somehow angered the society personnel who were serving as the conduit between the expedition and the press. Whatever the case, we believe that the apparent antipathy between the navy radio hierarchy and McDonald/Zenith, and the same situation at the National Geographic Society, caused historians to overlook the important role of McDonald and Zenith in the expedition and in communications history.

McDonald's motives for being involved in the 1925 MacMillan Expedition were misunderstood by many at the time, and that misperception has continued into the written record. Yet McDonald's motives for involving himself and Zenith in the earlier 1923–24 MacMillan expedition are clear. He was a very enthusiastic leader of the small regional radio manufacturer who wished to demonstrate the usefulness of the radio and his company to the general public. By supplying radios to the 1923–24 expedition and by broadcasting weekly to MacMillan (and not incidentally to most of the nation) from Zenith's powerful WJAZ, McDonald garnered priceless free publicity for his small company. Indeed, Zenith's first national print advertising campaign, which occurred that winter, prominently featured the connection between the company and the MacMillan expedition in every national advertisement. As a result, Zenith became a nationally recognized brand during the 1923–24 MacMillan expedition.

It has been commonly assumed that McDonald's motives for involvement in the 1925 expedition were the same: publicity and advertising copy for Zenith and, if McDonald could convince the navy to replace all of its longwave equipment with the new shortwave gear, a whole new market for Zenith Radio Corporation. This view of McDonald's motives does not match the facts. Although the expedition was a major national news event and Zenith received a measure of free publicity, virtually none of the extensive Zenith retail advertisements in 1925 even mentioned the expedition. Further, Zenith made it publicly known before the expedition sailed that it had no commercial interest in or plans related to shortwave. Indeed, the first radio that Zenith marketed that would tune shortwave frequencies did not reach the market until late 1933. Further, Zenith did no work for the military prior to World War II.

McDonald's motives, sadly, may seem naive to many modern readers: he was very patriotic and he loved the navy. Within a week of America's entry into World War I, he sold his multimillion dollar automobile business, banked the profits, and volunteered for the navy, accepting no salary for his service. During the war, he established a lifelong love affair with the navy. Certainly, one of McDonald's primary motives for his pivotal role in the 1925 MacMillan expedition was just as he stated it: to demonstrate the ability of shortwave radio to support reliable communications, day or night, over very long distances—a vital strategic communications link for the navy. McDonald also joined the expedition because he was an "adventurer." Though he never returned to the Arctic, McDonald went on to lead several archaeological expeditions and one major treasure hunting expedition in his later life. Part of his motivation for each of these expeditions seems to have been simply his desire for adventure in exotic locations.

McDonald's actions on the expedition appear to have been, by and large, honest and appropriate. He, like most of the other members of the group, exhibited conspicuous personal courage. His leadership in the planning of the expedition, during the frenetic preparations, during the coaling incident at Godhavn, and on the return journey, was vital to the expedition's success. His handling of the demotion and eventual removal of John Reinartz as chief radio operator also seems both just and appropriate to the facts. A less judicious man would have relieved Reinartz out of hand at Etah. Instead he was simply demoted. The fact that McDonald waited ten days after Reinartz's shocking and dangerous behavior while crossing Davis Strait before finally removing him also attests to McDonald's careful judgments in such matters.

McDonald's relations with Richard Byrd are much more difficult to characterize. In some ways, these two men were almost identical. Both had matinee-idol good looks; both developed early an intuitive grasp for manipulating the press and public relations to their own ends; and both appear to have had very high personal aspirations from a fairly young age. McDonald, however, developed a lifelong enmity for Byrd before or during this trip. It may be that these two similar and very large egos simply could not co-exist peacefully for ninety difficult days in such a small and crowded environment. Whether McDonald's behavior toward Byrd on the trip home was appropriate or whether he was "trying to get something on me" as Byrd clearly believed, is impossible for us to tell.

Reinartz

We were most troubled by the parts of our account describing the behavior of radio operator John L. Reinartz. This was partly because he was a more private man than was Byrd, McDonald, or MacMillan, and partly because the evidence of his misdeeds comes largely from the accounts and correspondence of McDonald, MacMillan, and the Chief Operator Gustafson at radio station 9XN, the powerful Zenith base station in Chicago.

John Reinartz may have sabotaged the stronger *Peary* transmitter on the way north so that his own transmitter aboard the *Bowdoin* would be the only contact with the outside world. While this would make no real sense in the world of commercial communications, Reinartz's stature in amateur radio would have been enhanced were he the only radio contact available on this exotic expedition. There is a slight chance that, instead of sabotage, it was Reinartz's technical incompetence that caused the problems and that his design and construction of the *Peary* transmitter was faulty. However, much less able radiomen than Reinartz (the *Peary* radio operators, McGee and Gray) found and fixed the problem quickly after Reinartz had spent considerable time while the expedition was on the Labrador coast supposedly doing so. McDonald chose not to remove Reinartz at that point, presumably because he had no proof of sabotage, only the opinions of Gray and McGee.

The record indicates that Reinartz ignored calls from both the powerful Zenith and navy transmitters on the way north while continuing to "DX" with his radio amateur colleagues. Raw messages back and forth between the expedition in Etah and the National Geographic Society and the navy in Washington indicate that some messages that Reinartz stated were "cleared" (confirmed as received at the far end) were not in fact received at the far end, if they were ever transmitted. This is a very serious offense. Still, we have only McDonald and MacMillan's personal correspondence charging that Reinartz lied about the affair.

Finally, Reinartz's failure to keep any part of his "each four hours" radio schedule while the *Bowdoin* crossed stormy Davis Strait on the way south is unconscionable. According to McDonald, Reinartz's only excuse for this lapse, when the *Bowdoin* finally reported in, was that he had been "seasick." Gustafson of 9XN, who saw Reinartz's log, later confirmed in writing that "seasick" was the only entry for several days. Reinartz's failure to keep any part of that radio schedule materially endangered the lives of every person on both ships. Had the overloaded *Peary* ventured out in storm-tossed Davis Strait in search of the "lost" *Bowdoin,* as McDonald was preparing her to do, there is every chance that she would have foundered and been lost with all hands.

While seasickness can be terribly debilitating, Reinartz's behavior must be contrasted against that of the entire tradition of shipboard radio operators, many of whom over the course of history gave their lives to tap out one last SOS call as their ships sank or burned around them. His behavior must also be viewed in the context of the ethical canons of the radio amateurs' organization from which he was chosen for the expedition. The American Radio Relay League was founded on the principle that the message must get through, even under the most difficult circumstances. Indeed, to this day, one of the two legislative rationales for the continued existence of "the amateur radio service" is its long history of often being the last communications link remaining when disasters strike. Reinartz simply did not uphold the standards of the ARRL.

As we first became aware of his career early in our research, we wondered why Reinartz disappeared so suddenly from the national radio amateur scene after the 1925 expedition. In the three years prior to the expedition, he wrote brilliantly and often in ARRL's magazine *QST,* discussing both circuit design and long-distance radio wave propagation. Even today, Reinartz is remembered as one of the fathers of amateur radio; his achievements, including the first shortwave transatlantic operation (along with Fred Schnell) and the design of one special direct conversion receiver circuit (the Reinartz circuit) are widely known. After the MacMillan expedition returned, he was never published again by *QST,* and at the age of thirty-one, dropped entirely from the radio amateur scene for several decades.[1] Evidently, ARRL President Hiram Percy Maxim and *QST* editor K. B. Warner felt the evidence of Reinartz's inappropriate actions during the MacMillan expedition was convincing. It is evident that Fred Schnell, who remained a friend of McDonald throughout his life, felt the same way.

Byrd

During our research we have often noted parallels between aspects of the 1925 MacMillan Arctic Expedition and Richard E. Byrd's two massive Antarctic expeditions of the Depression era (1928–30, 1933–35). It is obvious that Byrd profited a great deal from being included in this seminal modern expedition. In response to the terrible danger and cold that he and his men experienced in the single-engine, open-cockpit Loenings, it appears that Byrd never again flew in polar regions in an airplane with less than two engines. He preferred Fokker and Ford trimotor aircraft. Byrd also carefully exploited his participation in the 1925 expedition, his first moment of fame, by managing to have his own article for *National Geographic* published in the same issue (November 1925) as Commander MacMillan did.[2] From that point on, Byrd would dominate the stage and the spotlight of polar exploration.

There is ample evidence that Byrd profited from his experience on the MacMillan expedition in less obvious ways as well. Prior to MacMillan's 1923 expedition, there does not appear to have been a significant tradition of seeking commercial and industrial support for polar expeditions. McDonald's exploitation of Zenith's connection to the MacMillan 1923 expedition and its profound impact on the future of Zenith Radio Corporation was surely noted by other businessmen. Unfortunately, McDonald's files for this aspect of the 1925 expedition have not survived. However, it is known that Johnson and Johnson supplied the emergency first-aid kits for the planes and probably most other medical supplies gratis. Campbell Soups supplied much of the food, Bell and Howell supplied movie cameras and film, and Jensen Company supplied the outboard motors for the expedition skiffs. Even the survival knives carried by the flyers were contributed by Michigan-based Marble Knife Company.[3] Jensen Company (speakers) and Thordarsen (transformers), both Chicago-based electronic parts manufacturers, also supported the 1925 expedition. These manufacturers, of course, exploited their association with MacMillan—"the famous Arctic explorer"—and his 1925 expedition in advertising and point-of-sale displays. When Richard

Byrd began his campaign for financial support for his large expeditions to the Antarctic, he followed and expanded that same pattern.[4]

Byrd also seems to have profited from his observation of McDonald's mastery of radio broadcasting as a means to galvanize public opinion. By his second Antarctic expedition, Byrd was hosting a weekly radio show, broadcast over shortwave to North America and then carried over the CBS Radio Network nationwide.

While Byrd's drawing upon the experience and successes of those who preceded him is natural, neither he nor any of his biographers to date have mentioned even in passing the great debt that he owed to both MacMillan and McDonald for this aspect of his education. Byrd's grasp of modern media and modern marketing strategies was far less "intuitive" than was previously known.

It would be very easy for us to characterize some of Byrd's actions before and after the expedition as dishonest and self-serving. However, at least some of his actions need to be seen in the context of the times. In the spring of 1925, Byrd was trying to raise rather large amounts of money for his own expedition. The record is clear that he lied to the Fords and Rockefellers when he stated that he already had support from the National Geographic Society; he had not yet even asked for it. While this is not the behavior standard expected of a Naval Academy graduate or a Virginia gentleman, it is understandable and perhaps forgivable. In the first half of this century, the government was unwilling to fund major exploration or most attempts at various "world records." Each of the polar explorers had to be part hero, part huckster, part lecturer/scholar, and part carnival showman, if he was to raise the funds necessary for these large-scale, long-endurance expeditions. It can be argued that more reticent, less flamboyant explorers like MacMillan could never have raised the funds for the long, well-equipped expeditions that were necessary to explore the Antarctic.

Byrd's "private" accusations that MacMillan "came to town, learned our plans and then adopted them as his own" are much more difficult to understand or excuse. Byrd's accusations, currently accepted as fact, have continued to affect at least the details of the history of Arctic exploration. Byrd's own correspondence shows that he was still actively promoting a dirigible/ blimp flight to the Pole as late as three days before the fateful 28 March meeting where he officially learned of MacMillan's amphibian-based plans— which had been presented to Admiral Moffett and Secretary Wilbur a month earlier. Indeed, since the first written evidence of Byrd's plans to use amphibious, fixed-wing aircraft was dated that same day, 28 March, it seems likely that Byrd was, in fact, attempting to do what he accused MacMillan of doing: trying to steal another man's plans and expedition.

The incident at the Glynn Mill Inn where McDonald accused Byrd of listing his rank as "vice admiral" will forever remain a mystery. Byrd wrote that he thought "a friend had done it as a joke." It seems improbable that Byrd would have claimed a false rank in the very public hotel register, as McDonald accused him of doing. Some men serving under him on this and later expeditions greatly admired Byrd; others did not. The most likely explanation of the "vice admiral" incident is that one of his own men maliciously added the spurious rank.

We must also note the closing comment about Richard Byrd made by Eugene F. McDonald Jr. in one of our most singular sources, a 1948 letter to Robert F. Weinig, then a Zenith vice president at the Zenith plant in Iowa. Weinig had met Byrd at a banquet. Byrd had asked Weinig to act as an intermediary with McDonald to "patch up their differences," something that McDonald was very unwilling to do. McDonald's reply to Weinig explained his reasons in detail and closed with:

> It is a fact that we had trouble with Byrd on the entire expedition, but that trouble did not originate from the cause that Byrd indicates [the confusion over the second-in-command issue]. Our principal trouble with Commander Byrd was that he wanted to report having accomplished feats that we never attempted.

All of Byrd's apparent misdeeds must, however, be viewed in the light of his positive behavior, demeanor, and accomplishments during most of this expedition. His unquestionable personal bravery and determination to complete the mission of the Naval Arctic Unit virtually leap from the pages of the record. The flying on this expedition, with a new type of airframe and

an experimental and temperamental single engine, was surely more hazardous than any of his more famous flights. He led by example and conspicuous personal bravery. We must also note that he was very generous to
the men serving under him in his official dispatches and reports to the navy.
He was very careful to make sure that the men of the unit received full credit
for their own courage and steadfastness under very trying circumstances.
We hope that modern readers, who grew up, like we did, with Admiral Byrd
as a childhood hero, can accept the fact that Richard Evelyn Byrd was very
human, while we do not wish to forget or even diminish at all his pivotal
role in exploring and preserving for future generations the vast and largely
pristine Antarctic continent.

The Men of the Naval Arctic Unit

Finally, we must comment on the stellar performance of Lt. (j.g.) Meinrad
A. Schur, Chief Boatswain Earl E. Reber, and the men of the Naval Arctic
Unit. They served above and beyond the call of duty in the finest traditions
of the United States Navy. Late in our research, we came across a fragment
of what appears to have been a special expedition report to the National
Geographic Society. Clearly, Byrd wrote it in his capacity as commanding
officer of the Naval Arctic Unit. He spoke to the behavior of the men under
his command far more eloquently than we ever could:

> Operation facilities were naturally terrific—but we expected that. Comman-
> der MacMillan and all hands helped us at the start. In spite of all handicaps
> —working in the open, barehanded, exposed at times to snow and sleet—
> the disassembled planes were taken from the ship to the beach, erected and
> flown in three days.
>
> There were only six aviation men with me—Lt. Schur, Chief Boatswain
> Reber and Chief Petty Officers Bennett, Sorensen, Nold and Rocheville and
> then there was Francis, the Chief Aerographer. I consider the rapidity with
> which they got those planes into the air almost superhuman. That same
> spirit of efficiency characterized their work throughout. That is the reason
> we were able to fly over six thousand miles with the three planes in the
> Arctic Regions.

Many times I felt quite useless for the Unit did not need a Commanding Officer to tell them what to do. The biggest job I had was to make them stop working and get some sleep and rest. But in spite of me, they many times worked all night and reported ready to go the next day. These fellows took out of the planes three 900 pound Liberty motors and put three new ones in their place.

I still don't see how they did it. And when it came to flying over Ellesmere Land, where a forced landing meant "curtains" they were eager to go. I am proud of them and their courage and what they accomplished even though we did not reach the objective. Only actual flights up there could give the world knowledge of flying conditions in that part of the Arctic. Those flights have [now] been made and the conditions we found to be much worse than had been anticipated. We know now from considerable flying and a hard battle with the Arctic elements just what a flyer up there is up against . . .

As far as the ice and land was concerned, most of the time that the planes were over Ellesmere Land, a faulty engine would have meant a forced landing and a complete washout. All the ice was very rough.

Yet in spite of the landing conditions and the risky weather and the pitifully short operating time, the men with me, flew all together five thousand three hundred miles on the work of accomplishing the mission out over Ellesmere Land, 30,000 square miles were seen from the planes.

Looking back over the experiences of the 1925 MacMillan Arctic expedition, the largest mystery remaining is why these brave souls did not perish—a risk they faced not once, but many times over—during that summer and fall.

The aerial exploration at Etah was surely some of the most perilous non-combat flying ever undertaken. Going aloft with a new airframe and an untried inverted single engine, over some of the most rugged topography on the planet, was more than tempting fate. The engines in all three aircraft failed in the air; there was less open water to land on in the Etah vicinity than at any other time in living memory; and none of their navigational instruments worked properly. These brave flyers should not have lived to tell the tale.

The series of storms that struck the two vessels on their return voyages was one of the most vicious in the long sailing history of those waters. The

Peary was almost unimaginably overloaded with a very high deck load—one that also offered a great deal of wind resistance. Other ships foundered nearby. She probably should have turned turtle and gone down, but she did not. The *Bowdoin* was a tight and seaworthy boat, though she was badly overloaded until MacMillan put his own deck load of navy aviation fuel ashore at Hopedale. The historical record is full of similar Grand Banks and Labrador schooners going down with all hands as they were returning to port in the late fall season overflowing with cod. MacMillan's own father was lost in these waters on a similar schooner. But the *Bowdoin* survived.

They all survived.

Many of the players in the short intense drama that was the 1925 MacMillan Arctic Expedition went on to play prominent roles in the history of the next three decades. They made significant contributions in geographic exploration, aviation, and radio—and in World War II.

Lt. Cdr. Donald B. MacMillan

MacMillan continued making annual trips to the Arctic until he was eighty. In all, he made thirty-one Arctic voyages, many, in later years, with students from Bowdoin College. During World War II, he was assigned to the Hydrographic Office as an expert geographer of the Arctic regions. His beloved *Bowdoin* was commissioned in the U.S. Navy and served in the Arctic throughout World War II. In September 1954, at the age of eighty, MacMillan was promoted from commander to rear admiral on the eve of his thirtieth trip to the Arctic. He received many medals and awards, including the Peary Expedition Medal, the National Geographic Society's Hubbard Gold Medal, the Explorer's Club Medal, and the Elisha Kane Medal. He was elected to the Florence Nightingale Institute of Honorables for "successful endeavors to improve physical and mental conditions of the Eskimos." He died in September 1970 at the age of ninety-five.

Lt. Cdr. Eugene F. McDonald Jr.

McDonald never returned to the Arctic but he continued to pursue life as an adventurer. In 1928, he led an archaeological expedition to Isle Royale and organized the efforts that resulted in its designation as a national park in 1931. In 1930, while on a major treasure cruise to Cocos Island in the Pacific off Nicaragua, he discovered and befriended a starving recluse couple attempting to build a utopian paradise in the Galapagos Islands. The story was carried in the worldwide press. McDonald also led an expedition in 1930 to study early Native American artifacts on Georgian Bay and attempted to raise the Chevalier de La Salle's boat *Griffin*, sunk in 1679 in Lake Huron.

Thanks to McDonald's leadership, Zenith Radio Corporation came out of the Depression far stronger than it had entered; it would rise to be a major force in the rapidly developing electronics industry. McDonald died in 1958 and was posthumously inducted into the Broadcast Pioneers Hall of Fame. Among the accomplishments listed in the citation were his roles as founder, president, and first chairman of the board of Zenith Radio Corporation. The citation also listed his dynamic merchandising strategies, his inventions and innovations, his role as explorer, and his role as the first president of the National Association of Broadcasters. In addition, he was cited for having established one of the nation's pioneer broadcast stations, WJAZ, and for fostering the development of shortwave radio, international communication, ship-to-shore, FM, VHF, and UHF television, radar, and subscription television. Although an inventor, innovator, and marketing genius in the heyday of radio and television, today McDonald is the least known of the communications pioneers.

Lt. Cdr. Richard E. Byrd

Byrd became one of the world's best-known and most prolific explorers. He was recognized, possibly falsely, as having flown over the North Pole in a heavier-than-air craft on 9 May 1926. In 1927, he made a transatlantic flight thirty days after Lindbergh's flight. He led a large, privately funded Antarctic expedition between 1928 and 1930 during which he became the first person to fly over the South Pole. The massive Second Byrd Antarctic Expedition made major contributions to our scientific and geographic understanding of Antarctica. During that expedition, Byrd attempted to stay the winter alone at an advanced scientific base near the South Pole and nearly died of carbon monoxide poisoning. These two Byrd Antarctic Expeditions formed the basis for America's leadership position in Antarctic affairs for the next half century. Returning from his second expedition as one of America's most celebrated media stars and explorers, Richard E. Byrd provided leadership for three other large Antarctic expeditions before his death on 11 March 1957.

Rear Adm. William Moffett

Admiral Moffett's interest in naval aviation was already strong when he became chief of the Bureau of Aviation in 1921, and it grew ever stronger— and more influential—until his death in the crash of the dirigible USS *Akron* in 1933. Moffett possessed a rare combination of skill, political savvy, and drive that enabled him to build naval aviation during its crucial early years. He championed the causes of aircraft builders, flyers, and smooth procurement, and fought for the recognition of the navy's air branch as equal to its sea branch. He is considered by most historians to be the father of naval aviation. Moffett Field, south of San Francisco, was named in his honor.

Lt. (j.g.) Meinrad A. Schur

"Billie" Schur had set a number of world air speed records prior to the 1925 expedition. The navy, recognizing his unusual qualities as a pilot, used him as a flight instructor for most of his career. Soon after the Arctic expedition, Schur was assigned to the complement of the USS *Saratoga*, while she was under construction, to train navy pilots for deck landings. While on duty with the *Saratoga*, he was instrumental in developing the hook used on carrier deck landings. He was transferred to Hawaii in 1929, and while serving at Pearl Harbor, was the territorial governor's pilot. While in command of Patrol Squadron Four, he lead a formation of nine of the squadron's large multi-engine seaplanes on an eleven-hour, 840-mile flight that was recognized as the first aerial circumnavigation of the Hawaiian Islands. During his career, Schur seemingly made an avocation of rescuing downed flyers and others in distress. His most spectacular feat was the daring rescue of two downed army pilots while he was stationed in Hawaii. His bravery in this rescue was recognized with the Navy and Marine Cross. He was a member of the Quiet Birdmen. Later transferred from Hawaii to Long Beach, he helped to put Terminal Island Base in commission. Schur served in a flying capacity during most of World War II. He was seriously injured in a plane crash in the western Pacific and died on 6 December 1944.

Chief Boatswain Earl Reber

Earl Reber served most of the remainder of his long navy career on the West Coast, serving in flying capacities with the fleet and in seaplane-based patrol squadrons while stationed in San Diego and Pearl Harbor. Because of his skills as a flyer, he was also selected for duty at the Naval Aircraft Factory. In July 1928, Reber set five world speed records for Class "C" seaplanes. In 1929, he was involved with the testing of a dirigible trapeze which was designed to allow a dirigible to deploy its own fighter escorts from within the hull, and then recover them in midflight. In October of that year, Reber successfully flew a small Vought fighter aircraft through a series of midflight hookups with the trapeze then fitted to the dirigible USS *Los Angeles*. In 1937, while serving with Patrol Squadron Four in Hawaii, he was retired from the navy after being found physically incapacitated for service-related reasons. In 1943, Earl Reber was recalled to active service as a navy lieutenant, serving as an air operations officer at a training base near San Diego.

Floyd Bennett

Aviation Pilot Floyd Bennett received a commendation from the secretary of the navy in November 1925 for his work on the MacMillan Arctic Expedition. In 1926, he was the pilot for Lieutenant Commander Byrd on the flight that was recognized at the time as the first to reach the North Pole. For his service on that flight, Bennett received the Distinguished Service Medal and the Medal of Honor. Bennett toured forty-four American cities in the same plane used to make the 9 May 1926 flight to the North Pole. He was selected by Lieutenant Commander Byrd to be second in command of his first Antarctic expedition. Before the expedition departed, however, Bennett contracted pneumonia while flying to the relief of the first attempted westbound transatlantic flight. He died on 25 April 1928. As a tribute to Bennett, Byrd named the plane he used to fly over the South Pole *Floyd Bennett,* and on reaching the Pole, dropped an American flag that was weighted with a stone from Bennett's grave. A major civilian airfield, later to serve for many years as a naval air station, was named Floyd Bennett Field in his honor.

Grover Loening

Grover Loening received the first master's degree in aeronautical engineering given from Columbia University in 1908, the first person in America to receive such a degree. He served for a number of years as a personal assistant to Orville Wright before returning to New York in 1917 to establish Loening Aeronautical Engineering Corporation in Manhattan to manufacture aircraft. His pioneering Loening Amphibian, first used on the 1925 MacMillan Arctic Expedition, was later used by the army, navy, marines, and Coast Guard, and by airlines and private owners all over the world. After building Loening Aircraft into a very successful specialized aircraft manufacturer, he merged his company with Curtiss-Wright in 1928. Loening eventually left Curtiss-Wright and established his own very successful aeronautical design consulting practice. He numbered among his clients Curtiss-Wright, Grumman Aircraft, Fairchild, Chase Bank, and many others. During this same time, Loening served as a pioneer director of Pan American Airways.

Grover Loening's contributions to American aviation were enormous and were recognized by the National Aeronautical Association in 1950, when he became only the third recipient of the Wright Brothers Memorial Trophy (the first two recipients of the trophy were Dr. William F. Durand and Charles Lindbergh). He also received the Air Force Medal in 1955 and the Guggenheim Medal in 1960 for "a lifetime devoted to the development of aeronautics in America." Grover Loening also wrote many books and articles about early aviation. It is interesting to note that, during the development of the Loening Amphibian, Roy Grumman was Loening Aircraft's plant supervisor. Grumman went on to design and manufacture some of the most successful navy aircraft ever built, under his own name and corporation.

Kennett Rawson

Fourteen-year-old cabin boy and able seaman aboard the *Bowdoin*, Kennett Rawson returned to Chicago after the 1925 expedition and wrote the book, *A Boy's Eye View of the Arctic*, while completing his sophomore year of high school. He accompanied MacMillan Arctic expeditions to the Far North during the summers of 1926, 1927, and 1929, becoming an excellent polar navigator in the process. Immediately after his graduation from Yale in 1933, he was selected as the navigator for the Second Byrd Antarctic Expedition. Following his return from the Antarctic, he worked in the editorial department of G. P. Putnam's Sons, a New York publisher. During World War II, Rawson served in the navy, first as a navigator and later as a commanding officer. He was awarded the Navy Cross, America's second highest honor for valor. Rawson returned to G. P. Putnam's after World War II, eventually serving as a vice president and editor in chief. In 1950, he left Putnam's to serve as president of David McKay Co. Inc., another New York publisher, for twenty-four years before founding his own publishing house, Rawson, Wade, Publishers. He was a lifelong and very active member of the Explorers Club in New York.

Arthur Collins

The fifteen-year-old Cedar Rapids radio amateur received a great deal of publicity when his homemade equipment allowed him to be in contact with the expedition, often at times when others were unable to reach it. Collins began selling radio equipment of his own design in 1930. His approach to circuit and cabinet design was immediately successful and in 1933 he incorporated as Collins Radio Company. His company specialized in amateur and military equipment and became one of the nation's largest. Rockwell International bought Collins Radio in the mid-1970s and, as Rockwell-Collins, the company continues today supplying the professional and military markets with sophisticated telecommunications equipment.

A True Copy of Letter from E. F. McDonald Jr. to Hon. Curtis D. Wilbur

February 28th, 1925
Hon. Curtis D. Wilbur
Secretary of the Navy
Navy Department
Washington, D.C.
My dear Mr. Secretary,

In compliance with your suggestion, I am submitting this letter in confirmation of our conversation of this day.

Our call, as you know, was prompted by our interest in the Navy and in our close personal friend, Donald. B. MacMillan, D. Sc. now Lieutenant Commander in the United States Naval Reserve Forces. Dr. MacMillan is a professor in Anthropology on leave for exploration purposes from Bowdoin College. Commander MacMillan served with our naval forces during the late war in aviation, entering the service as an enlisted man and obtaining his commission at the expiration of the war.

MacMillan had spent seventeen years of his life in Arctic exploration. His next trip, this June, will be his ninth back into the Arctic, and I feel that I am safe in my statement that no living white man knows the Arctic better than MacMillan. His first trip was with Admiral Peary on his successful expedition to the Pole and it was MacMillan who was selected by Peary from his whole crew to be the one man to accompany him on the final dash, but MacMillan unfortunately froze his feet and was sent back by dog sled.

MacMillan headed the Crocker Land Expedition that went into the Arctic intending to stay only one year and it was on this expedition that MacMillan proved his wonderful generalship, when forced to stay four years, he brought all his men out in excellent condition. It was on this expedition that MacMillan removed from the maps Crocker Land and proved it be, if you please, a permanent mirage.

It is the writer's belief that this year, among other things, MacMillan will write and prove the first chapter in American History, as he has discovered off the Coast of Labrador ruins that have every indication of being the ruins of the Norsemen of about 900—?—A.D. on an island known as Turnivik. MacMillan's work in the Arctic has been purely scientific, following the lines of Anthropology, Ornithology, Glaciology, Mineralogy, Meteorology, Tidal Observations and Geographic; and he has also done an enormous amount of work in Terrestrial Magnetism, the records of which are now in the hands of the Carnegie Institute of Washington. Most of his crews in the past have been made up of scientists and college men.

MacMillan has done a great humanitarian work among the Esquimaux. He is a man of the highest principles and morals, and has done much in cultivating the friendship of the Esquimaux, to such an extent that the Esquimaux now express a desire to be citizens of the United States and under our rule rather than that of Denmark or any other foreign countries.

Other countries, especially England, when private exploring expeditions leave, place the commanders in the Naval Reserve of their respective country and order them to active duty. Admiral Peary's expedition was a private expedition but Peary, then Commander, was on active duty for the United States Navy when he planted our flag at the North Pole. Exploration primarily is and has been in the past Navy work and in the future should be Navy work. You will recall that by an act of Congress, funds were appropriated that sent Wilkes for the Navy Department into the Antarctic. The first American Arctic expedition was financed and sent out by Congress in about 1850 under the Command of Lt. De Hadin [*sic*; McDonald was likely referring to the DeLong expedition], the second under Dr. Elisha Kent Kane, surgeon in the U.S. Navy and on active duty.

Our call today was not for the purpose of asking for funds. This is a private scientific expedition, but a great work may be done and the United States, through the Navy Department, would receive the credit. MacMillan's expedition to the Arctic this year is a trip of only four months duration—June to September inclusive. He owns his own ship, his expedition is financed, but his work can be greatly broadened in scope by the use of an amphibian plane with which he can explore the interior of Baffin's Land, the interior of Axel Heiberg Land, the interior of Ellesmere Land, and the interior of Northern Greenland where exists the great Greenland Ice Cap which is yearly pouring out an avalanche of icebergs. These interiors, except for small sections, have never, so far as records show, been seen by human eye. Enormous lakes may be mapped, mineral deposits may be found, unknown shore will be delineated. To use verbatim the words of MacMillan, more work can be done with an aeroplane in a period of days than has been done by all the Arctic explorers with their dog teams in the past hundred years. There also exists between the North Pole and Point Barrow a great unexplored area of over one million square miles, in which by tidal observations and other indications MacMillan is strongly led to the belief there exists a continent.

Ice conditions permitting, it may be possible to move the *Bowdoin*, which will be MacMillan's mother ship for the plane, to a base far enough north to possibly explore a small section of this unexplored area, though the real work in this land must be done sooner or later with the lighter than air craft as was approved by President Coolidge in his letter to the Secretary of the Navy, late in 1923. Unquestionably greater and more accurate work in mapping can be done by lighter than air and larger personnel, but this proposed expedition of this summer with the one plane which we are asking of you, is merely the first step to do for the United States what will be done by foreign governments if we do not move rapidly. Right at this moment Amundsen has $100,000 contributed to him by a Mr. Ellsworth of New York City for the purpose of flying over the Pole with two Italian built machines. This is another case of American capital financing a foreign enterprise.

You spoke today of the hazard. It is true the hazard is greater than flying over civilization, but not to a marked degree.

In conclusion, our desires are to have Doctor MacMillan assigned to active duty, the Navy department to order a plane, a pilot, and one mechanician to accompany the expedition at no additional expense to the Navy.

If for any reason you do not approve of ordering the plane and the two men to accompany the expedition, will the Navy Department rent to the

MacMillan Expedition an amphibian to leave with it in June, the expedition to employ its own mechanician and pilot?

If neither of the above proposals have your approval, it is our intention to purchase a plane, if one can be built in time, and we will be glad to give the Navy Department the opportunity to supervise and advise in the construction of this plane for this work, because we know that future development of Navy planes must be along those lines, and we have every confidence in the Navy to produce the best. We fully realize the importance of the work that can be done by airplanes in the Arctic.

Even though we are forced to purchase the plane and make this purely a private expedition, we will still welcome the ordering of Doctor MacMillan to active duty.

I want you to know that Commander Isbester and myself appreciate the interest that you evidenced today and in our discussion with Admiral Moffett we found that we were working along pretty much the same lines as the Navy. Admiral Moffett is intensely interested and we pointed out to him that the great Middle West is today still wondering why the proposed *Shenandoah* trip never materialized.

We pointed out to Admiral Moffett that if the Navy, through Congress, is not permitted to send the *Shenandoah* next year, we will be glad to, with private interests, finance a lighter than air expedition.

As we all know, Canada arbitrarily lays claim to all lands north of Canada, explored or unexplored, and we have sat passively by offering no objection in the past because of the supposed uselessness of this land, but with progress of planes and dirigibles in the past ten years a new value now presents itself and if there is undiscovered land in the Arctic, it should be under the United States flag and though we ourselves used it for mooring masts or bases it is too quickly accessible from Europe and from Asia for hostile operations against us from the air.

As you know, Steffansson acting for Canada tried to lay claim to Wrangle Island and he has been trying to get stepping stones for the British Government in this polar area for future air work, just as the British have stepping stones all over the ocean for their fleet.

Incidentally you remarked that you had read "Steffansson." I am taking the liberty of mailing you under separate cover, with my compliments, a copy of "Four Years in the White North" by MacMillan. I sincerely trust you will pardon the appearance of this old copy, but the edition is out of print and I was forced to secure this copy from a second-hand bookstore.

Time is short. We must move rapidly, in order to leave in June, and we want you to know, My dear Mr. Secretary, that we will appreciate your timely consideration.

Thanking you, I am

Sincerely yours,

E. F. McDonald, Jr.

EFM: c

Authors' note: The original was an onionskin author's copy of this letter, McDonald files, Zenith Archives.

Personnel of 1925 MacMillan Arctic Expedition

Lt. Cdr. Donald B. Macmillan, in command.

Lt. Cdr. E. F. McDonald Jr., second in command.

Lt. Cdr. R. E. Byrd, in command Naval Flyers.

Schooner *Bowdoin*

Lt. Cdr. Donald B. MacMillan, Captain
  Freeport, Maine

Ralph F. Robinson, Mate
  Merrimac, Mass.

John J. Jaynes, Engineer
  Somerville, Mass.

John Reinartz, Radio Operator
  Manchester, Conn.

Onniga Melkon, Sailor (and Photographer)
  South Waynesmouth, Mass.

Martin Vorse, Cook
  Somerville, Mass.

Richard Salmon, Sailor
  Larchmont, N.Y.

Kennett Rawson, Sailor
  Chicago, Ill.

Edward Goding, Pilot
  Boston, Mass.

Maynard Owen Williams, Photographer and Writer
  National Geographic Society
  Washington, D.C.

Benjamin H. Rigg, Magnetic Observer
  Ideas and Currents

U.S. Coastal Geodetic Survey
Burlington, N.J.

Steamship *Peary*

Lt. Cdr. E. F. McDonald Jr., in command
Chicago, Ill.

Geo. F. Steele, Captain
Roxbury, Mass.

U. J. Herrmann
Chicago, Ill.

Hosmer L. Freeman, Mate
South Weymouth, Mass.

W. D. Publicover, Chief Engineer
West Somerville, Mass.

Paul J. McGee, Radio Operator
Matoon, Ill.

P. N. Davidson, 1st Asst. Engineer
Portland, Maine

Edward MacNamara, Seaman
East Boston, Mass.

William Parker, Fireman
New Orleans, La.

Henry King, Seaman
Cambridge, Mass.

Adolph Harloff, Cook
North Boston, Mass.

E. Freel, Fireman
South Boston, Mass.

Van R. Brown, Fireman
Charleston, Mass.

John Kenney, Messman
Roslindale, Mass.

Rufus Sewall, Officer's Mess
Wiscasset, Maine

John MacNamara, Seaman
Everett, Mass.

Dr. L. M. Davidoff, Physician
Peter Bent Brigham Hospital
Boston, Mass.

Harold R. Gray, Radio Technician
Chicago, Ill.

Jacob Gayer, Staff Photographer
National Geographic Society
Akron, Ohio

Walter N. Koelz, Zoologist
University of Michigan with
U.S. Bureau of Fisheries

U.S. Naval Contingent Attached to ss *Peary*

Lt. Cdr. R. E. Byrd, in command, USN
Winchester, Va.

Lt. M. A. Schur, USN
Nashville, Tenn.

Chief Boatswain E. E. Reber, USN
Millville, N.J.

N. P. Sorensen, ACM, USN
Menominee, Mich.

Albert Francis, C., Aerog, USN
San Francisco, Calif.

C. F. Rocheville, AMM 1/c, USN
Coronado, Calif.

A. C. Nold, ACMM, USN
South Bend, Ind.

Floyd Bennett, USN
Waterbury, Vt.

The 1925 MacMillan Expedition and
the Court-Martial of Col. Billy Mitchell

Just as the expedition participants dispersed across the United States to resume their normal lives, the country was swept up in the court-martial of American air power's most famous and controversial figure, Col. Billy Mitchell. The trial began on 28 October 1925, two weeks after the expedition landed at Wiscasset. Colonel Mitchell had long been known for his highly provocative public statements disparaging the army's and especially the navy's leadership regarding military aviation. His latest and most vitriolic public statement, released in September 1925, was the immediate cause of his trial.

Mitchell's statement was triggered by two incidents involving naval aviation. On 3 September 1925, while the MacMillan expedition was at Holsteinsborg, Greenland, the navy's dirigible, uss *Shenandoah,* was destroyed while on a goodwill flight over Ohio, with the loss of fourteen lives. Two days previously, a navy flying boat was thought to have been lost on an attempted nonstop flight from San Francisco to Hawaii. From his exile post in Texas, Mitchell issued a six-thousand-word denunciation of the Navy and War Departments, saying that these and other accidents were "the result of incompetency, criminal negligence, and the almost treasonable negligence of our national defense" by those departments. Mitchell added, "All aviation policies, schemes and systems are dictated by the non-flying officers of the Army and Navy, who know practically nothing about it." Mitchell also criticized the MacMillan expedition's use of Loening Amphibians under Lieutenant Commander Byrd, calling them "jitneys—unsuited for Arctic flying because they were designed for the Tropics." He ended his diatribe by saying, "I can stand by no longer and see these disgusting performances . . . at the expense of the lives of our people, and the delusions of the American public." The reaction to Mitchell's remarks was swift. He was placed under technical arrest and ordered to Washington for court-martial.

On 5 October, while the *Peary* lay in Halifax harbor awaiting the *Bowdoin,* Byrd received orders directly from the secretary of the navy separating him from the expedition and turning command of the Naval Arctic Unit over to Lt. M. A. Schur. Byrd was ordered to "PROCEED IMMEDIATELY WASHINGTON D.C. RESUME DUTY BUREAU OF AERONAUTICS." He arrived less than two weeks before the trial and began preparation for his testimony in defense of naval aviation.

Both the Navy Department and expedition participants were very concerned as to who else would be called to testify to rebut Mitchell's charges. Correspondence between McDonald and MacMillan in later years indicates that McDonald, Congressman Britten, and others worked vigorously behind the scenes to assure that Lieutenant Commander MacMillan would not be subpoenaed. All knew that MacMillan would testify, based on the expedition's experience, that he believed that fixed-wing aircraft were unsuitable for use in the Arctic. This testimony, of course, would be highly embarrassing to the navy and could be interpreted to bolster Mitchell's charges. MacMillan was not called to testify. The Schur family relates that the Navy Department also was worried about the possibility that Lieutenant Schur, known for his bluntness, would be subpoenaed. Eventually, Schur was subpoenaed but did not testify at the trial.

In the end, the defense of the navy's part in the expedition fell on the capable shoulders of Lieutenant Commander Byrd, who defended the use of the "jitney" Loening aircraft with the able assistance of the designer-manufacturer himself, Grover Loening.[1] Byrd's questioning by Assistant Trial Judge Advocate Major Gullion (one of the attorneys for the army prosecution of Mitchell) was very thorough. His questions allowed Byrd to provide a positive view of the planning and preparation for the expedition. Gullion also questioned Byrd extensively about the selection of the Loening aircraft for the mission. Again, Byrd described the Loenings as the most appropriate aircraft, emphasizing the performance of the planes in the extremely hazardous flying conditions that summer and stating that ". . . we gave the planes a good trial and they did very well. No other plane, an amphibian, could have flown as many miles as we did this summer." Byrd's cross-examination by Mitchell's lawyer, Senator Reid, was rambling and often veered from the subject. At times Reid's questions actually bolstered the navy's case rather than that of his client. Reid cross-examined Byrd extensively as to whether the planning and preparation for the expedition was hurried; Byrd insisted that it was not.

One section of Lieutenant Commander Byrd's testimony during Reid's cross-examination seemed to the court-martial Law Member (judge) and both attorneys to be odd, irrelevant, and out of place. Reid was leading Byrd through the planning of the MacMillan expedition:

Q. What was the next step in your preparations?

A. The next step was in March when they called for volunteers for the MacMillan expedition.

Q. Who put out that call?

A. I was trying to get an expedition up of my own—not of my own, but with Capt. Robert Bartlett. We finally concluded we would take planes rather than airships, the heavier-than-air planes would be better than airships to go to Etah, because you could not get there until August and the winds are bad in August and it would not do for airships and we decided on heavier-than-air planes. Capt. Bartlett and I decided we would ask for Loening planes and we asked the Navy Department for two Loening planes.

Byrd clearly was not telling the truth. He actually abandoned the dirigible-based expedition with Bartlett in late March because Goodyear finally told him it would not give him the blimp envelope he needed. Further, his claim that he knew ahead of time about weather conditions at Etah and that he knew that no expedition could reach Etah until August do not match the written record. As late as Battle Harbor on the journey north, Byrd thought it normal to reach Etah in early July, having been so misinformed by Fitzhugh Green. Whatever Lieutenant Commander Byrd's motives, it is obvious that he wanted this version of the events of that March to be in sworn public testimony, whether or not it was relevant to the question asked and whether or not it was correct.

Byrd's comments were so out of context with the proceedings that the next three pages of the court-martial transcript are taken up with the two attorneys and the Law Member trying to decide why Byrd himself brought up the Byrd/Bartlett expedition. They felt it was clearly irrelevant to the question asked him and eventually decided to let the matter drop; Reid moved on to other matters.

With the exception of this one curious exchange, Byrd's testimony describing the expedition, while given in as positive a light as possible, was straightforward and truthful and served the navy, naval aviation, and the expedition very well.

At the close of Byrd's testimony, Grover Loening was called to the stand. Colonel Mitchell's statements that the Loening Amphibians were "jitneys— unsuited for Arctic flying because they were designed for the Tropics" are among his most curious charges. As detailed in chapter two, Mitchell himself was intimately involved in the development and procurement of the Loening Amphibians for the army.

Grover Loening was concerned and upset by Mitchell's allegations about the amphibian. The very survival of Loening's small aircraft company depended upon the acceptance of those aircraft in military aviation circles. There is some indication that Loening asked to be called as a witness for the prosecution.

As to Mitchell's charge that the Loening Amphibians were "jitneys," Senator Reid again failed himself and his client during his cross-examination of Loening by asking: "Was yours the greatest amphibian ever built?" Loening replied, "So General Mitchell said before the President's Board and I agree with him."[2]

Loening was referring to Mitchell's sworn testimony before a special board convened by President Coolidge to investigate all aspects of procurement of aircraft by the military. Senator Reid must have been shocked by the answer.

Both sides also questioned Loening at length as to whether the Loening Amphibian was "designed for the Tropics" as Mitchell charged. It is clear from the testimony that, though the army planned to deploy the Loenings first in Hawaii and Panama, they were not designed for any particular climate and were thought by Loening to be suitable for all climates. Loening testified that the Loenings had been used in a series of demonstration flights during very bad winter field conditions of ice and snow at Bolling Field in Washington in January 1925. Many army, navy, and congressional figures, including Mitchell, visited Bolling Field to view the amphibian. Loening testified that Mitchell himself suggested that the hull shape of the amphibian should allow it to land on soft snow without skis. He added that they (Mitchell and Loening) went on to discuss, positively, using the aircraft in Alaska and above the Arctic Circle.

Unquestionably, Col. Billy Mitchell was a visionary and one of the most influential leaders in the history of military aviation. However, the testimony of Byrd and Loening showed that all of Mitchell's charges related to the 1925 MacMillan Arctic Expedition were without merit. The court-martial of Billy Mitchell finally closed after seven weeks of testimony. The board only deliberated for half an hour before voting to convict on the charge of insubordination and all eight specifications. Colonel Mitchell resigned his commission in February 1926. With the close of the court-martial and Mitchell's resignation, the 1925 MacMillan Arctic Expedition under the auspices of the National Geographic Society passed from the stage of history.

Chapter 1. *Early Arctic Exploration*

1. Eric Newby, *The Rand McNally World Atlas of Exploration* (New York: Rand McNally & Co., 1975), 243.

2. Seventy-five years later, after hundreds of thousands of Arctic miles and Arctic service throughout World War II, the *Bowdoin* still makes journeys north as a Maine Maritime Academy training vessel.

3. Probably the first use of radio in polar regions should be attributed to the Australian Antarctic Expedition led by Sir Douglas Mawson between 1911 and 1914. The expedition established sporadic wireless communications with Australia that greatly helped in breaking down the group's feeling of isolation. A detailed account of the expedition and the role radio played is found in Sir Douglas Mawson, *The Home of the Blizzard: The Story of the Australian Antarctic Expedition, 1911–1914* (South Australia: Wakefield Press, 1996).

Chapter 2. *Planning the First Modern Expedition*

1. MacMillan to Moffett, 5 October 1924, found in RG 72, Records of the Bureau of Aeronautics, Records of Division and Offices within the Bureau of Aeronautics, Office Services Division, Administrative Services, General Correspondence, A-11 (1) Vol. 1, Box 788–89, Entry 62. These records contain much of the official correspondence for the expedition.

2. MacMillan to Moffett, 22 January 1925.

3. To the U.S., the national sovereignty of the lands in the Far North was still very much in question in 1925. As plans for the MacMillan expedition became more public, Canada, in a 15 June 1925 letter to Secretary of State Frank Kellogg, expressed concern that MacMillan would be flying over Canadian land without first asking Canada's permission. As proof of its sovereignty, Canada informed Kellogg that the Royal Canadian Mounted Police had established posts in Baffin and Ellesmere Islands, as well as a number of other areas in the Far North. The letter stated that, "Legislation formally requiring scientific or exploring expeditions to secure such permits before entering any part of the Canadian northern territories was enacted by both Houses of Parliament this month." There was a vigorous exchange of letters over the next month between the State Department, the navy, and the Canadian government. The U.S. government

took the position that if the expedition asked permission, it would be official recognition that Canada indeed owned the northern lands.

4. Though never before publicly known, the surviving expedition records indicate that there was no attempt to obtain major funding for the expedition other than that provided by the National Geographic Society and the immensely wealthy McDonald. Evidently, if the navy was unable or unwilling to provide the expedition with an aircraft, McDonald was prepared to rent or buy one himself. Likewise, when the navy was reluctant to provide a physician, McDonald provided one at his own expense.

5. Hale's response to McDonald (7 March 1925) also mentions arranging a "moving picture matter." This "matter" developed into an invitation for MacMillan to present a talk to the entire cabinet in late March. See McDonald files, Zenith.

6. Byrd to R. A. Bartlett, c/o Explorers Club, New York, 24 February 1925, found in R. A. Bartlett papers, Hawthorne-Longfellow Library, Bowdoin College.

7. Byrd Archives, the Ohio State University Libraries.

8. Letter on stationery from the National Geographic Society, Byrd Archives, the Ohio State University Libraries.

9. Byrd Archives, the Ohio State University Libraries.

10. Byrd to the secretary of the navy, 28 March 1925, Byrd Archives, the Ohio State University Libraries.

11. McDonald to Hon. Curtis C. Wilbur, 4 April 1925, McDonald files, Zenith.

12. According to a 1 April letter from Isbester to Moffett, the first that anyone associated with the MacMillan expedition knew of Byrd's plans was the meeting in Moffett's office on 28 March 1925.

13. The agreement MacMillan signed with the National Geographic Society on 20 April contained a clause requiring the first public talk after the expedition to be made by MacMillan at the National Geographic Society. There were also clauses about ownership of photographic and story rights. Byrd signed a statement agreeing to these clauses on 18 April, eight days after writing this letter to Green.

14. Byrd Archives, the Ohio State University Libraries, Folder 4236.

15. Meinrad A. Schur was born in Marshfield, Oregon, and joined the navy in 1912. He entered naval aviation in December 1916, serving as officer in charge of aviation at Dunwoody Naval Training School, Minneapolis. From January 1918 to January 1919 he was a flight instructor at the Naval Air Station, San Diego, and from October 1921 to May 1923 he served as a pilot in aircraft squadrons with the Battle Fleet and then as a flight instructor at the Naval Air Station, Pensacola. During this time he flew in a number of air races representing the navy and on 2 October 1923 won second place in the Merchant's Exchange Trophy Race in St. Louis. He also was a participant in the navy flight to Panama. He was serving in Pensacola when assigned to the MacMillan Arctic Expedition in April 1925.

16. Earl E. Reber was born in Chicago, Illinois, on 2 January 1888 and joined the navy as a boatswain (temporary) on 15 November 1917. On 12 February 1924 he was ordered to Washington as part of the Arctic expedition of the *Shenandoah*. He was

serving at the Aircraft Factory, Navy Yard, Philadelphia, when selected for the MacMillan Arctic Expedition. The rank "aviation pilot" was a designation in the navy of that era of a noncommissioned officer pilot.

17. Floyd Bennett was born in Warrenburg, New York, on 25 October 1890 and enlisted in the navy on 15 December 1917. In September 1924 he was ordered to the cruiser *Richmond* to conduct landing site reconnaissance in Greenland for the army around-the-world project. He was transferred to the Naval Air Station, Anacostia, for duty with the MacMillan expedition in April 1925.

18. Andrew C. Nold was born at Nappanee, Indiana, on 16 September 1895. He enlisted in the navy in May 1917 and was sent to the Naval Air Station, Pensacola, for aviation training. In November 1924 he received the rating of aviation pilot and was selected for the MacMillan Arctic Expedition in April 1925 while at Anacostia.

19. Nels P. Sorensen was born at Menominee, Michigan, on 11 April 1890 and enlisted in the Naval Reserve Force at Great Lakes, Illinois, in December 1917. In August 1923 he was assigned to the Naval Air Station, Anacostia, where he was on duty when assigned in April 1925 to the MacMillan Arctic Expedition.

20. Charles Francis Rocheville served in the navy from October 1914 to February 1915. In August 1918 he enrolled in the naval reserve force at Los Angeles and in July 1920 was recalled to active duty and placed in the regular navy. In February 1924, he was selected as one of the enlisted men to take part in the never-conducted Naval Arctic Expedition on the dirigible *Shenandoah*. He was transferred to Naval Air Station San Diego in March 1925 and to the MacMillan Arctic Expedition in April 1925.

21. In fact, Amundsen, along with the American Lincoln Ellsworth, jumped off from Kings Bay, Spitzbergen, on 21 May 1925 at 5:00 P.M. By 1:00 A.M., they were within 136 miles of the Pole when a shortage of fuel forced them to turn back. An almost fatal mistake was made when they landed in a small open lead to converse and get their bearings for the return flight. One of their two "Whales" (Vals) was badly damaged on landing and the Ellsworth crew almost lost their lives trekking over fresh thin ice to reach the other seaplane. The lead closed around the second ship and only the crew's superhuman effort got her up on the ice floes. For most of the next month, the party faced slow starvation as they struggled to smooth and solidify a runway on the ice floe so that their now badly overloaded Val could take off. During much of the preparation for their own expedition the MacMillan party seriously considered the idea of changing their plans to a search for the Amundsen party. Only by the narrowest of margins did the Amundsen party finally take off, on 18 June, and return to Spitsbergen to surprise a waiting world. Needless to say, the Amundsen party had no radio equipment with them. The MacMillan party learned by radio of Amundsen's reappearance and kept to their original plans.

As a contingency, the commanding officer of the *Shenandoah* provided a suggested rescue plan for the Amundsen-Ellsworth Expedition on 26 May 1925. The very detailed plan, never used, is found at the National Archives, Records of the Bureau of Aeronautics, Records of Division and Offices within the Bureau of Aeronautics, Office

Services Division, Administrative Services, General Correspondence, A-11 (1) Vol. 3, Box 788–89, Entry 62.

In 1926, Amundsen and Ellsworth reached the North Pole on the dirigible *Norge* piloted by the Italian commander Umberto Nobile. Their flight took them across the Pole to northwest Alaska, slicing the unexplored area neatly in half and proving conclusively that no major landmasses were to be found there. It has long been assumed that the *Norge* was twenty-four hours too late to claim the Pole, Byrd and Bennett having beaten them flying a multi-engined plane out of Spitsbergen. New evidence strongly suggests that Byrd and Bennett had missed the Pole and should not be credited as the first to reach it, the honor perhaps going to Amundsen, Ellsworth, and Nobile. No radios were used by either party.

Two years later, Nobile organized his own airship-based expedition to the Arctic (Crocker Land, again) and was reported lost. Roald Amundsen, the first man to reach the South Pole, organized one more expedition in an attempt to find Nobile. He, five other men, and their airplane disappeared into the frozen wastes of the Arctic; no one has ever learned their fate. A few days later Nobile was rescued, partly due to a very small radio transmitter that survived the crash of the dirigible.

22. The speed of change in radio technology was brought home by McDonald and MacMillan's experiences on the 1923–24 expedition. The two years of 1923 and 1924 saw stunning developments in all phases of radio from the understanding of the physical principles of signal propagation to the techniques of network broadcasting. When MacMillan went north in the spring of 1923, he had been pleased to carry the most modern Zenith "shortwave" equipment with him. By the time the Canadian Coast Guard ship *Arctic* came up to Etah and Refuge Harbor in the summer of 1924, radio science had redefined those Zenith radio sets as operating on "medium wave" (around 1 MHz). The *Arctic*'s radio operator noted that had the *Bowdoin*'s radios been shortwave, they could have communicated over longer distances. (The *Arctic* transmitter used frequencies around 2.4 MHz, then defined as shortwave, now defined as within the medium-wave spectrum.)

23. Taylor's eight-page "white paper," "Short Waves and the Polar Flight of the *Shenandoah*," written on 12 February 1924, details his philosophy and the status of the current knowledge of high-frequency radio. In this paper, he speculates on how radio communications from the 1923 MacMillan Expedition might have been improved.

Chapter 3. *The Expedition Sails North*

1. See later incidents and Reinartz section in the afterword for a discussion of this problem.

2. It was letters from these isolated Labrador missionaries and possibly letters from a few of their brethren in Greenland, all rather desperate for more batteries, that eventually led McDonald and Zenith into the Wincharger business to electrify America's rural areas with the power of the wind. Typical of McDonald, even in internal Zenith

publications, he did not speak of letters from missionaries, only of "friends in the North."

3. Two possible reasons for this damage were found in different locations in the written record. One version blames the prop's striking one of the brass fittings of the *Peary*'s swamped lifeboat during her grounding outside Hopedale. The other version blames a large *Bowdoin* deck hawser that became entangled in her prop at some point. Both incidents may have happened.

4. Documents of the time refer to the waters between the northern shore of Labrador and the southwestern coast of Greenland as "Davis Strait." Modern atlases refer to these waters as the Labrador Sea; they call the somewhat more restricted seas north of there, between southern Baffin Island and the Greenland coast, Davis Strait.

5. The expedition operated on "75th meridian time." This is roughly equivalent to Eastern Standard Time and to the approximate local time of their destination at Etah.

Chapter 4. *Etah at Last*

1. Ten pigeons and their shelter charged to Chief Aerographer Albert Francis were taken to Etah for messenger service between downed aircraft and the base at Etah. After an acclimation period, the birds were released on 7 August. They were immediately terrorized and confused by the "millions upon millions of little auks." Only four pigeons returned from the initial release and after several other test flights only three remained. Francis attributed the loss to the presence of gerfalcons, which would have found pigeons easy pray. Francis recommended in a 13 August report to Byrd that the remaining three birds be returned to the U.S. Naval Air Station at Anacostia. Byrd agreed and in Francis's final report, dated 12 November 1925, he indicated that the pigeons and the remainder of their food had been returned to the navy. It is interesting to speculate on the navy's need to include pigeons in the communication mix.

2. R. E. Byrd, "Flying over the Arctic," *National Geographic*, November 1925.

3. Byrd's General Order Number One to the Polar Unit indicated the materials that must be carried by each plane while flying. The very detailed list was broken down as follows:

Food for one month	180 lbs
Tools	15 lbs
Miscellaneous	325 lbs (which included the 90 lb. radio set)

Additionally, the planes carried:

Weight of two men	340 lbs
180 gallons of gasoline	115 lbs
20 gallons oil	180 lbs

General Order Number One states that with a total weight of 5,755 pounds, the planes should have a cruising radius of 675 miles at twenty-four gallons per hour and should be able to drop five hundred pounds of extra material for each trip to the base 150 miles distant.

4. The sun compass was invented for this expedition by Albert H. Bumstead, head of the National Geographic Society Cartographic Department. The compass consisted of a twenty-four-hour watch with only the hour hand. Bumstead reasoned that since the sun circled the region in twenty-four hours, laying the watch so that twenty-four o'clock pointed at the Greenwich meridian would cause the hour hand to follow the sun. When flying, the hour hand was to be kept toward the sun; it would not only indicate time but also the direction. Unfortunately, this device proved to be of little use to the aviators, since they never climbed above the upper cloud deck and thus never saw the sun. Bumstead filed for a patent on the Bumstead Compass in 1926. *National Geographic* Press Release, 28 May 1925, *National Geographic* Archives. Bumstead to Byrd, 1 December 1925, Byrd Archives, the Ohio State University Libraries, Folder 4237.

5. One of these two operators was a young amateur, Gilbert Gustafson, who went on to be chief engineer and vice president for engineering during Zenith's glory days.

6. *QST* magazine, the official organ of the ARRL, covered the activities of the 1925 expedition and is one of the primary sources commonly available to casual readers. Caution should be exercised in assuming that the *QST* reports, and indeed the operators' logs, are a complete record of the expedition's radio activities. They are not complete. Every single nonpublished source that we have accessed—the papers of McDonald, MacMillan, and Schur—document numerous instances of nonradio amateur uses of the equipment that are not shown in the operators' log books.

Chapter 5. *Southbound For Home*

1. D. B. MacMillan, "The MacMillan Arctic Expedition Returns," *National Geographic*, November 1925.

2. Ibid., 515.

3. Although this *National Geographic* press release attributes this story to MacMillan, it could not have been him, since he had not yet arrived at Godthab. Additionally, the McDonald files in the Zenith Archives contain a radiogram from McDonald to MacMillan informing him of the incident. The detailed information in this press release surely came from McDonald and not MacMillan.

4. Memorandum from Byrd signed by the Naval Unit, 27 September 1925. Byrd Archives, the Ohio State University Libraries, Folder 4232. It is not known whether this memorandum was ever passed forward by Byrd or if it was constructed as a safety measure. Hundreds of documents in the McDonald files attest to the friendly and life-long relationships McDonald maintained with all members of the Arctic Unit except Byrd. In several cases, documents show that McDonald was still sending gift television sets every Christmas to the widows of the Arctic Unit officers and men thirty years after the expedition.

5. Rawson is incorrect in referring to the ladies having joined the ships at Battle Harbor. They met the expedition at Monhegan Island as indicated by numerous news reports.

Afterword

1. John L. Reinartz, who died in October 1964, reappeared posthumously in a December 1964 article in the ARRL magazine *QST* titled "First Maxim Medal Awarded to Reinartz." The two-page biography was largely drawn, the article relates, from a biography printed in souvenir programs given at Reinartz's retirement dinner (from Eimac Corp.) in 1960. The 1960 biography is wildly inaccurate as far as Reinartz's connection to the Arctic, mentioning only Byrd's 1926 flight to the Pole while almost certainly referring to the 1925 MacMillan Expedition. It appears that Reinartz misrepresented his own history in this 1960 biography, perhaps to more closely associate himself with the very famous Admiral Byrd or to mask his participation in the 1925 MacMillan Arctic Expedition. Byrd had died in 1957 and McDonald in 1958, but Admiral MacMillan was very much alive.

A more accurate biography, at least as far as the 1925 expedition is concerned, appeared in the August 1981 issue of *Ham Radio* magazine. This nine-page article, "John L. Reinartz, Father of Shortwave Radio," was written by Leonard Spencer, WA6CBQ, with the assistance of Reinartz's widow. The article devotes two pages to the 1925 expedition and is relatively accurate as to the positive elements of Reinartz's duties with the expedition. As one would surmise, the article makes no mention of Reinartz's demotion at Etah or of his removal as a radio operator on the way home.

2. Historically, polar explorers had financed their ventures through lecture fees and royalties deriving from magazine articles and books written about their adventures. The common pattern was for each expedition member to sign a contract with the expedition leader forgoing all lecturing or writing about the adventure. Thus, the leader could maximize fees and royalties to pay off expedition debts and generate funds for the next expedition. Byrd had pressed for permission to write about the 1925 expedition, and the navy leadership, seeing publicity for the cause of naval aviation, had supported him in this.

3. The Johnson & Johnson, Campbell Soups, and survival knife support was related in a telephone conversation between Virginia Glendening and John H. Bryant. The Jensen outboard and parts manufacturer participation may be seen in contemporary advertising and photographs.

4. One of the support arrangements made by Byrd caused at least thoughts of mutiny on the Second Antarctic Expedition. Byrd contracted with the manufacturer of Kool cigarettes to the effect that Kool cigarettes, supplied by the manufacturer, would be the only tobacco products allowed on expedition vessels or at Little America

on the Antarctic Ice Shelf. This arrangement was very unpopular with all the smokers on the expedition, especially those who preferred to smoke pipes. From a private communication from an expedition seismographer, Glenn H. Bryant, to John H. Bryant.

Appendix D

1. Byrd and Loening testified on 1 December 1925. Their testimony appears on pages 2103–81 of the official trial transcript, which may be found in the Special Collection of the Libraries at the U.S. Air Force Academy.

2. The only definitive work on the trial of Billy Mitchell written since the transcript of the trial that has been available to scholars is a dissertation from Rutgers University titled *Trial of Faith: The Dissent and Court-Martial of Billy Mitchell* by Michael L. Grumelli. One of the major points of this work is that, though Mitchell certainly was guilty of the insubordination charges brought against him, his defense led by Senator Reid was extraordinarily inept. Grumelli makes a convincing case that many of Mitchell's charges could have been shown to have had at least some basis in fact by a more astute defense.

BIBLIOGRAPHY

Archives

The primary sources for our research have been the documents, both official and personal, created by the participants at the time of the 1925 MacMillan Arctic Expedition and their correspondence in subsequent years. The more important of these documents and their sources are identified in the notes. These documents were found in the following locations:

National Archives, Washington, D.C.
The archives contain official correspondence related to the 1925 expedition, particularly in its early planning stages, as well as planning documents for the proposed 1924 *Shenandoah* expedition. These papers have been available for inspection by scholars for many years.

Hawthorne-Longfellow Library and Peary-MacMillan Arctic Museum, Bowdoin
College, Brunswick, Maine
The library contains the papers of Rear Adm. Donald B. MacMillan and Arctic sailing captain and explorer Robert Bartlett. MacMillan's personal diary of the 1925 expedition and his correspondence with Eugene F. McDonald Jr. were particularly useful. These papers have been available to scholars since the early 1980s.

McDonald Files, Zenith Archives, Chicago, Illinois
The McDonald files, which we discovered and are in the process of organizing, were very important to our work. These papers have not previously been available to anyone.

Byrd Archives, the Ohio State University Libraries, Columbus, Ohio
Rear Adm. Richard E. Byrd's personal diary, his collection of official papers related to the 1925 expedition, and, especially, his copies of his own correspondence, were key to establishing the source of some of the distortions of history that we document in our manuscript. These papers have been available to scholars only since 1995.

Papers of Cdr. Meinrad A. Schur, Schur Family, Lakewood, California.
The Schur papers were the source for much of our depiction of the human dimension of the expedition in its early days. They were also the source for many of the photographs used in this book. These papers have not previously been available to anyone.

National Geographic *Archives, National Geographic Society, Washington, D.C.*
As a cosponsor of the expedition, the National Geographic Society files contained key press releases as well as some very important correspondence.

Papers of the Navy Historical Center, Department of the Navy, Washington, D.C.
The personnel of the Navy Historical Center were especially helpful in providing background documentation concerning the careers of the members of the Naval Arctic Unit and in advising us on the probable location of other navy records related to the expedition.

Books and Other Published Material

A number of texts were useful in providing background material and in documenting some aspects of our work. The primary texts referenced in our manuscript are:

Allen, Everett S. *Arctic Odyssey: The Life of Donald B. MacMillan.* New York: Dodd, Meade and Co., 1962.

Cones, Harold, and John Bryant. *Zenith Radio: The Early Years, 1919–1934.* Atglen, Pa.: Schiffer Publishing, 1997.

Department of the Navy. *Toward the Poles: A Brief Account of Polar Expedition.* Washington, D.C.: U.S. Government Printing Office, 1950.

DeSoto, D. B. *Two Hundred Meters and Down.* Rev. ed. Newington, Conn.: American Radio Relay League, 1981.

Erngaard, Erik. *Greenland: Then and Now.* Copenhagen: Landemann Ltd., 1972.

Grossnick, Roy A. *United States Naval Aviation, 1910–1995.* Washington, D.C.: Naval Historical Center, 1997.

Grumelli, Michael L. "Trial of Faith: The Dissent and Court-Martial of Billy Mitchell." Ph.D. diss., Rutgers University, 1991.

Howeth, L. S. *History of Communications-Electronics in the United States Navy.* Washington, D.C.: U.S. Government Printing Office, 1963.

Loening, Grover. *Amphibian.* Greenwich, Conn.: New York Graphic Society, 1973.

———.*Our Wings Grow Faster.* New York: Doubleday & Co., 1935.

Newby, Eric. *The Rand McNally World Atlas of Exploration.* New York: Rand McNally, 1975.

Rawson, Kennett. *A Boy's Eye View of the Arctic.* New York: Macmillan, 1926.

Vaughan, Richard. *Northwest Greenland: A History.* Orono, Maine: University of Maine Press, 1991.

Periodicals and Newspapers

Articles from a number of popular magazines and newspapers from the era were useful and provided key information in a number of significant areas. Some of these sources are documented in the notes section.

INDEX

Italics indicate photographs or maps.

ABOUT THE AUTHORS

John H. Bryant, FAIA is a professor of architecture and former head of the
School of Architecture at Oklahoma State University. He is also a former
senior Fulbright research scholar to Japan and is a well-known authority on
the ancient architecture of East and South Asia.

Professor Bryant has lectured internationally on architectural topics as
well as on his second love, the history of radio. He has coauthored three
other books on radio and has written numerous articles on that topic.

In researching *Dangerous Crossings*, Professor Bryant continued exploring two other lifelong interests: the history of aviation and the history of
polar exploration. His interest in the latter springs from the fact that his
father was a seismographer on Richard E. Byrd's Second Antarctic Expedition in the mid-1930s.

Professor Bryant was recently elevated to the College of Fellows of the
American Institute of Architects in recognition of his contribution to the
education of architecture students, practicing architects, and the general
public. He and his wife of thirty-five years, Linda, divide their time between
residences in Oklahoma and the San Juan Islands north of Seattle.

Harold N. Cones, Ph.D, is a professor of biology and longtime chairman of
the Department of Biology, Chemistry and Environmental Science at
Christopher Newport University. He also is an instructor in the International Elderhostel program through Virginia Commonwealth University's
Virginia Center on Aging. For many years, Dr. Cones has also been associated with the Mariners' Museum in Newport News, Virginia, where he con-
ducts ecotours and is an educational and environmental consultant.

Dr. Cones has had a lifelong interest in shortwave radio listening and lectures and teaches often on that topic. He has published widely in the tech-

nical and popular press and has authored two manuals and coauthored or authored four books, two of them on radio history.

Dr. Cones is the recipient of five teaching awards and was recently selected as a Virginia Outstanding Professor. His other interests include commercial archaeology, old-time radio programming, travelling, and writing. He and his wife, Linda, have been married for thirty-five years and reside in Newport News, Virginia.

Professor Bryant and Dr. Cones have previously collaborated on two other books on radio history: *The Zenith Trans-Oceanic: The Royalty of Radios* and *Zenith Radio: The Early Years, 1919–1935*. In 1998, Professor Bryant and Dr. Cones received the Houck Award from the Antique Wireless Association for their contribution to the history of radio.